TIME
FOR KIDS
BIG
BOOK OF
WHEN

TIME For Kids
Managing Editor, TIME For Kids Magazine: Nellie Gonzalez Cutler
Creative Director: Jennifer Kraemer-Smith
Project Editor: Andrea Delbanco

Time Home Entertainment
Publisher: Jim Childs
Vice President, Brand & Digital Strategy: Steven Sandonato
Executive Director, Marketing Services: Carol Pittard
Executive Director, Retail & Special Sales: Tom Mifsud
Executive Publishing Director: Joy Bomba
Director, Bookazine Development & Marketing: Laura Adam
Vice President, Finance: Vandana Patel
Publishing Director: Megan Pearlman
Assistant General Counsel: Simone Procas
Assistant Director, Special Sales: Ilene Schreider
Brand Manager: Jonathan White
Associate Prepress Manager: Alex Voznesenskiy
Associate Production Manager: Kimberly Marshall
Associate Project Manager: Stephanie Braga

Editorial Director: Stephen Koepp
Senior Editor: Roe D'Angelo
Copy Chief: Rina Bander
Design Manager: Anne-Michelle Gallero
Editorial Operations: Gina Scauzillo

Special thanks: Keith Aurelio, Katherine Barnet, Brad Beatson, Jeremy Biloon, Susan Chodakiewicz, Rose Cirrincione, Assu Etsubneh, Mariana Evans, Christine Font, Susan Hettleman, Hillary Hirsch, David Kahn, Jean Kennedy, Amy Mangus, Nina Mistry, Dave Rozzelle, Ricardo Santiago, Holly Smith, Adriana Tierno

For information on TIME For Kids magazine for the classroom or home, go to TIMEFORKIDS.COM or call 1-800-777-8600.
For subscriptions to SI Kids, go to SIKIDS.COM or call 1-800-889-6007.

Published by TIME For Kids Books,
An imprint of Time Home Entertainment Inc.
135 West 50th Street
New York, NY 10020

ISBN 10: 1-61893-043-5
ISBN 13: 978-1-61893-043-9
Library of Congress Control Number: 2013954647

TIME For Kids is a trademark of Time Inc.

Produced by Contentra Technologies
Project Manager: Himanshu Chawla
Writer: John Perritano
Designer: Rakesh Kumar
Photo Researcher: Nivisha Sinha

We welcome your comments and suggestions about TIME For Kids Books. Please write to us at:
TIME For Kids Books, Attention: Book Editors, P.O. Box 11016, Des Moines, IA 50336-1016
If you would like to order any of our hardcover Collector's Edition books, please call us at 1-800-327-6388 (Monday through Friday, 7 a.m. to 8 p.m., or Saturday, 7 a.m. to 6 p.m., Central Time).

1 QGT 14

Contents

How to Use This Book

When did people first pop popcorn? When was ice cream first eaten? When were video games invented? When did the dinosaurs go extinct? The *Big Book of When* answers these questions and many more you never thought to ask. In these 11 chapters, you will explore the solar system, find out when people first walked on the moon, and learn about the ruins of ancient civilizations. You don't have to read this book from start to finish—interesting questions appear in every chapter and on every page. Find a topic that most interests you and dive right in. Look at the glossary of terms and phrases to learn the meaning of words that appear in bold throughout this book.

Introduction: These give a brief background about the topic to help you understand both the question and the answer.

Special Features: *A Look Back* and *A Look Forward* tells you the history of the topic and take you into the future.

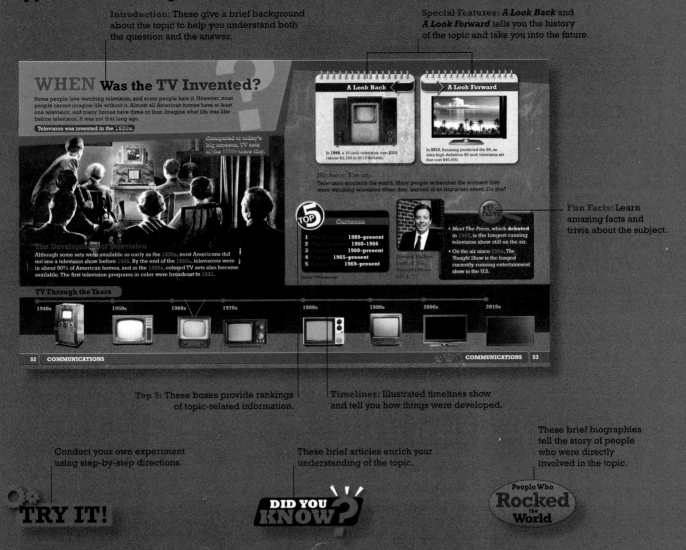

Fun Facts: Learn amazing facts and trivia about the subject.

Top 5: These boxes provide rankings of topic-related information.

Timelines: Illustrated timelines show and tell you how things were developed.

Conduct your own experiment using step-by-step directions.

These brief articles enrich your understanding of the topic.

These brief biographies tell the story of people who were directly involved in the topic.

TRY IT!

DID YOU KNOW?

People Who Rocked the World

The experiments and activities in this book require adult supervision. Time Home Entertainment Inc., TIME For Kids, and Contentra Technologies disclaim all responsibility and liability for any damage or injury caused or sustained while performing any of the experiments and activities.

WHEN Did Time Begin?

At some point early in life, most people learn how to tell time. It's a critical skill—understanding minutes, hours, days, weeks, months, and years is a big part of what keeps order in our society. When did we start keeping track of time like this?

World's oldest mechanical clock, 1380, Wells Cathedral, England

March of Time

Most often, we use clocks and calendars to measure time. We also measure time by the circular motion of the moon, Earth, and sun. It takes one month for the moon to go around Earth and one year for Earth to go around the sun. Every day, Earth spins on its **axis**, which makes it look like the sun is moving across the sky. We can measure the length of a day by following the shadows created by the sun.

FUN FACTS

- Daylight saving time began when Benjamin Franklin suggested that people could save candles by waking up earlier in the summer and working longer during daylight hours. Daylight saving time was formally adopted in the U.S. in 1918.

- To keep clocks in sync with Earth's slowing **rotation**, a "leap second" has to be added every few years.

WHEN Did People Begin to Use Calendars?

The oldest calendar was not like the one hanging on your wall. It was a row of ancient pits in Scotland that are about **10,000 years old**. Stone Age humans dug this complex series of holes to represent the months of the year and phases of the moon. They used that calendar for **6,000 years**.

Save the Date

Many ancient **civilizations** created their own calendars by tracking the motion of objects they saw in the sky, such as the sun, stars, moon, and planets. The Sumerians, who lived in what is today Iraq, created one of the world's first calendars **5,000 years ago**. It divided the year into 30-day months.

Other ancient calendars include:
• An ancient Egyptian calendar that marked time by a star in the **constellation** Canis Major. The star, which now goes by the name Sirius, rose next to the sun every 365 days.

Ancient Egyptian calendar

Aztec calendar

- The Babylonian calendar had 29-day and 30-day alternating months that equaled roughly 354 days. The Babylonians added three extra months every eight years.

- In 46 B.C., Julius Caesar, the ruler of ancient Rome, wanted to have one calendar that people could use across the Roman Empire. This calendar year was 365 days long, with one extra day (**leap day**) added every four years. Caesar moved the first day of the year from March 1 to January 1.

The Pope's Calendar

Today, most of the world uses the Gregorian calendar, named for Pope Gregory XIII. In the late 1500s, Pope Gregory wanted to align Easter with the first day of spring. As a result, his calendar year is exactly 365 days, 5 hours, 48 minutes, and 46 seconds long.

Pope Gregory XIII

World Calendar?

Can there be one common, logical calendar for the entire world? The so-called World Calendar was developed by an American woman named Elisabeth Achelis in the early 1930s. The World Calendar is similar to the Gregorian calendar, but it has some major differences. Each year in the World Calendar is divided into four equal quarters. Each quarter begins on a Sunday and ends on a Saturday. The Saturday following December 30 is called Worldsday—not December 31—and it is followed by Sunday, January 1. In leap years, another day is added to the month of June. Worldsdays do not have a month or a number, just the letter *W*. While the calendar has some support, it has never been adopted by any country.

WHEN Did Humans First Begin Measuring Time?

Humans first started to measure and record the passage of time about **30,000 years ago**. To do so, they recorded the phases of the moon.

Egyptian Minute

Historians credit the ancient Egyptians with dividing time into the hours and minutes we use today. They did this by using a simple sundial—a stake placed in the ground. They watched as the sun's movement changed the shadow of the rod's length and direction. Around 1500 B.C., the Egyptians built a more advanced T-shaped sundial that divided the period between sunrise and sunset into 12 parts. As years went by, the sundial became more advanced, making the marking of time much easier.

As the moon orbits Earth, it goes through several phases. Each cycle starts with the new moon and ends with the full moon.

1500 B.C.

Nighttime

How did people tell time when it was dark outside? Sundials can't work at night. To solve this problem, ancient Egyptians looked to the stars. They marked twilight to dawn by the appearance of 36 stars that divided the nighttime sky into 12 equal parts.

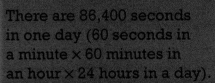

FUN FACTS

There are 86,400 seconds in one day (60 seconds in a minute × 60 minutes in an hour × 24 hours in a day).

WHEN Did People Start Using Clocks?

Not all clocks use numbers. Early clocks used a variety of methods to divide day and night into different periods.

6th–10th century

Water Clocks

A water clock measured time at night. Invented around **1500 B.C.**, these devices allowed water to flow into a container. As the water level rose, measurements on the container helped people determine what time it was.

Chinese water clock

Greeks began using water clocks about **325 B.C.**

Candle Clocks

During the 6th century in China and the 10th century in England, people kept time by watching candles burn. People marked lines on the candle so they could tell when each hour passed. Candle clocks gave an idea of the time, but they weren't that accurate because different waxes burn at different rates.

2h
3h
4h
5h
6h
7h
8h
9h
10h
11h
12h
13h
14h
15h
16h
17h
18h
19h
20h
21h
22h
23h
24h

Hourglasses

By the 1300s, **artisans** had mastered the art of glassmaking. Hourglasses helped people keep time by measuring the speed of sand as it moved from the top to the bottom of the glass.

1300

TRY IT!

How to Build a Sundial

What You Will Need

- pencil
- paper plate
- colored marker or crayon
- ruler
- plastic straw
- pushpins or tape

What to Do

Step 1

Use the pencil to poke a hole through the center of the paper plate. Write the number 12 on the inner rim of the plate with a colored marker or crayon. Use the ruler to draw a straight line from the hole in the center of the plate to the number 12. Add the numbers 1 through 11 at equal intervals, as shown.

Step 2

At exactly noon, take the plate and straw outside. Place the plate on a table or on the ground in the sun. Put the straw through the hole in the center of the plate. Tilt the straw slightly toward the line on the plate. Turn the plate so that the shadow of the straw falls along the line to the number 12.

Step 3

Using pushpins or tape, fasten the plate to the ground or table. Check the position of the shadow at 1 p.m. Put a check mark next to the number 1 on the inner rim of the plate where the shadow falls. Continue checking and marking the plate at the start of each hour. By the end of the day, you will have a completed sundial.

WHEN Did People Start Using Mechanical Clocks?

In the 13th century, European artisans designed the mechanical clock as a more reliable method of telling time. The earliest mechanical clocks were designed in Europe in the late 1300s.

For Whom the Bell Tolls

By 1300, workers were building clocks for churches in Italy. Prior to this, people told time by listening to the **tolling** of the church bells.

Early German watch with sundial

Portable Clocks

In the 1500s, only the rich could afford to have a clock in their home. Most people had to rely on church clocks or the sun to tell time. Then clockmakers found more efficient and less expensive ways to make **portable** timepieces that were more affordable to everyone.

All in Good Time

Gears help mechanical clocks keep time. Gears have two important parts: a mainspring and a **pendulum**. The mainspring tightens when you use a key to wind a clock. As the mainspring begins to unwind, its energy turns the gears. The gears cause the hands of the clock to move at the right pace. Some mechanical clocks use weights instead of a mainspring. When the weights pull on the gears, the hands of the clock move.

FU FACTS

Grandfather clocks were originally called longcase clocks. The name changed in 1876 when an American musician named Henry Clay Work wrote a song titled "My Grandfather's Clock."

Mechanical Clocks

What makes a mechanical clock tick? An **escapement** is at the heart of all mechanical clocks. For example, in a grandfather clock, an escapement makes sure that the clock's gears advance at a steady and equal rate. That's why the hands of the clock move forward with precision.

Big Ben, Houses of Parliament, London, England, completed in 1859

WHEN Were Time Zones Established?

In 1883, the U.S. became the first nation to use **time zones**. Before this, every town kept time by its own clock, using the sun to determine local time. Let's say you lived in Boston and your aunt lived in Worcester, a few miles away. Noon in Boston occurred three minutes before noon in Worcester. You set your watch three minutes ahead of your aunt in Worcester.

Give It a Try!

Look at the time zone map of the U.S. See if you can answer the questions below.

1. If it's 3 a.m. in Oklahoma, what time is it in Washington State?

2. When it is 9 a.m. in Alaska, what time is it in Hawaii?

3. How many time zones does Indiana have?

4. If you left Massachusetts at 4 p.m. and flew to Oregon, arriving 3 hours later, what time would it be in Oregon?

2:00 a.m. AKST

3:00 a.m. PST

4:00 a.m. MST

1:00 a.m. HST

5:00 a.m. CST

6:00 a.m. EST

■ Alaska Time Zone (AKST) ■ Pacific Time Zone (PST) ■ Mountain Time Zone (MST)
■ Hawaii Time Zone (HST) ■ Central Time Zone (CST) ■ Eastern Time Zone (EST)

ANSWERS: 1. 1:00 a.m. 2. 8:00 a.m. 3. two 4. 4:00 p.m.

All Aboard!

The railroad changed how everyone kept time. As railroads grew, so did the need for a uniform timetable for every stop along the line. Otherwise, people would miss the train.

1869 Union Pacific poster advertising the opening of the first U.S. transcontinental railway

WHEN Traveling from Japan to California, What Day Is It?

The International Date Line is an imaginary line that extends through the Pacific Ocean from the North Pole to the South Pole. If you're traveling from west to east and cross this line, you lose a day on the calendar. Sunday, for example, becomes Saturday. The opposite happens when you're traveling east to west.

Monument marking the International Date Line on the south coast of Britain

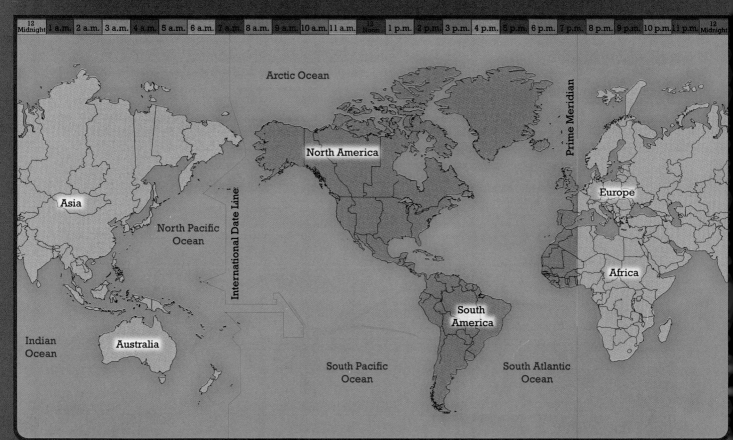

Map of the International Date Line

An Imaginary Line

One day, Keisha celebrated her birthday. The next day, her older twin brother Pedro celebrated his birthday. How is that possible? Keisha and Pedro's mother was traveling between Japan and California when she gave birth to the twins. Because Pedro was born first, he was older. But when their mother crossed the International Date Line, Keisha was born on the previous day.

Sunrise, Sunset

Portuguese explorer Ferdinand Magellan was the first to notice the loss of a day. He sailed around the globe in the 1500s. When he returned home, Magellan realized that when he traveled westward ahead of the setting sun toward the Pacific, he lost a day.

Mind Bender

If you flew two hours from the island of Tonga, which is west of the International Date Line, to Soma, on the east side of the line, you'd arrive 22 hours before you left.

WHEN Is a Day Complete on Other Planets?

The length of a day on a planet is determined by how fast it rotates on its axis. Since each planet rotates at a different speed, the length of a day on one planet can be much different from the length of a day on another planet. The length of a year is also different because each planet revolves around the sun at a different speed.

Neptune
Length of Day: 16.11 Earth hours
Length of Year: 164.79 Earth years

Mars
Length of Day:
24.62 Earth hours
Length of Year:
1.88 Earth years

Pluto
Length of Day:
6.38 Earth days
Length of Year:
248.54 Earth years

Saturn
Length of Day: 10.66 Earth hours
Length of Year: 29.46 Earth years

Uranus
Length of Day: 17.23 Earth hours
Length of Year: 84.01 Earth years

Mercury

Length of Day: 58.65 Earth days
Length of Year: 88 Earth days

Earth

Length of Day:
23.93 hours
Length of Year:
365.26 days

FU FACTS

- **Venus**
  A day on Venus is longer than a year.
  Also, Venus rotates counterclockwise.

- **Jupiter**
  Jupiter is the largest planet but has
  the shortest day.

- **Neptune**
  If you were 12 years old on Earth,
  you'd be 1,977 years old on Neptune.

- **Pluto**
  It takes sunlight 5.3 hours to
  reach Pluto.

Venus

Length of Day: 243.01 Earth days
Length of Year: 224.7 Earth days

Jupiter

Length of Day: 9.92 Earth hours
Length of Year: 11.86 Earth years

WHEN Do People Use Time Capsules?

A time capsule is a way for a current generation to tell a future generation about their lives. Time capsules are usually buried in the ground or hidden in vaults. Though they come in all shapes and sizes, these sealed containers hold items from a particular point in time. They typically contain a guided tour in the form of a letter explaining what each item is and why it was included. Imagine burying a time capsule for 2075. What would you put in it?

TIME CAPSULE
BURIED
December 29, 1999
TO BE OPENED
2100

Time in a Box

The Westinghouse Electric & Manufacturing Company coined the name "time capsule" for the 90-inch bullet-shaped container the company buried at the 1939 World's Fair in Flushing Meadows, New York.

City Hall, Venice, Florida

World's Largest Time Capsule

Harold Davisson of Seward, Nebraska, wanted his grandkids to know what life was like in 1975, so he built a 45-ton vault and buried it in his front lawn. He stuffed it full of toys, books, records, dolls, and clothes. He also included a whole car. The vault will be opened on July 4, 2025.

FUN FACTS

The Yahoo! Time Capsule captured the thoughts and feelings of the world in 2006 as an exercise in electronic or digital **anthropology**. When the time capsule was sealed on November 8, 2006, it contained 170,857 digital items including digital pictures, music, books, and movies. The capsule will be opened in 2020.

TRY IT!

Think about the things that you use every day that your grandparents, or even your parents, never dreamed about. What makes your life, your neighborhood, and this year unique? Make a time capsule of your very own.

Step 1

Pick a container with a lid, such as a mason jar or a coffee can.

Step 2

Fill it with whatever you want. Dated newspaper clippings are a good idea, as are photographs, ticket stubs, or vacation souvenirs. Write a short note explaining what is inside.

Step 3

Bury or hide the container. Put it in a closet, under a bed, or in the attic. You could also dig a hole and bury your time capsule in the ground. Write a letter that you leave outside of the capsule telling when you want the capsule to be opened.

WHEN Sharks Breathe?

Scientists determined that sharks existed some 200 million years before dinosaurs emerged. Sharks are among the oldest creatures on our planet. In Cleveland, Ohio, scientists have found **fossils** of sharks that are believed to be 400 million years old.

When Are Sharks Active?

People used to think that if a shark stopped moving, it could not breathe and would drown. This is only true for some sharks. Sharks remove oxygen from the water in order to breathe. Water enters the shark's mouth and flows around its gills. Inside the gills are hundreds of feathery **filaments** that contain blood vessels. These blood vessels absorb oxygen from the water as it passes by.

Keeping the Oxygen Flowing

In some sharks, muscles around their mouths pull water in and send it over the gills. It is a process called buccal pumping. The sharks that use this technique include the nurse, angel, and carpet sharks; they do not need to swim to breathe.

Other sharks are called obligate ram breathers; these sharks must swim or they will drown. About 24 shark **species**, including the great white and mako, are obligate ram breathers.

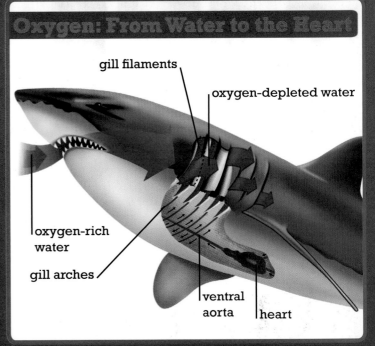

Oxygen: From Water to the Heart

gill filaments

oxygen-depleted water

oxygen-rich water

gill arches

ventral aorta

heart

Nap Time

It takes more effort for a shark to remain still than to swim. Because obligate ram breathers are constantly on the move, they sleep very little. But because scientists can't watch every shark every second of the day, it is hard to know whether sharks take short naps. It is possible that they are able to shut off their brains and rest while they are still swimming.

WHEN Did Alligators Appear?

Alligators can be traced back some **200 million years**. They managed to survive while their contemporaries, the dinosaurs, died off.

When Do Alligators Hibernate?

Alligators thrive in Florida. They can be seen on golf courses, in swamps, swimming pools, and even parking lots. It seems like they never sleep, but they do. Alligators **hibernate** in the winter when the temperature dips below 70°F. They carve a little den in the mud and sleep until it gets warm.

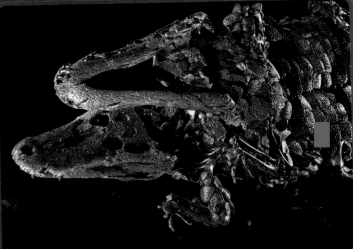

This **49 million-year-old** alligator fossil was found in Germany.

Lazy Hunters

Alligators do not actively hunt other animals. Instead, they wait in the water for an unsuspecting animal—a turtle, a bird, a fish, or even a deer—to pass by. When the meal is within reach, the gator pounces with amazing speed. Once it catches its **prey**, the alligator drags the unlucky animal under water and drowns it. An alligator's jaws are so powerful that it can crush a turtle's shell into bits.

Webbed feet

Alligators vs. Crocodiles

- **Home:** freshwater habitats
- **Jaws:** U-shaped
- **Teeth:** When they close their mouths, their teeth are hidden.

- **Home:** freshwater and saltwater habitats
- **Jaws:** V-shaped
- **Teeth:** When they close their mouths, you can see a toothy grin.

Armored body with a muscular tail

Up to 80 teeth

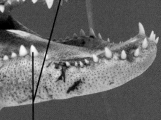

Claws

WHEN Did Dinosaurs Die Out?

Scientists believe that some **65 million years ago**, a giant asteroid or comet, about 6.21 miles (10 kilometers) across, slammed into what is today the coast of Mexico. It came without warning, fast and furious—a streaking bright light blazing across the sky. The impact of the asteroid changed the face of Earth. Dense clouds of dust and rock darkened the sky, chilling Earth's surface. The change in climate killed most living things, including dinosaurs.

The first dinosaur bone was identified in 1822. Since then, scientists have found more than 1 billion dinosaur fossils of different shapes and sizes. These ancient relics indicate that at least 300 different kinds of dinosaurs once walked the planet.

When Dinos Ruled

Humans have been around for only 4.5 million years, starting 61 million years after dinosaurs vanished. The age of the dinosaur can be broken into three different periods.

240 to 205 million years ago

Triassic

- About 240 million years ago, the earliest dinosaurs appeared.
- The first Triassic dinos were small and fast. They ate meat and walked on their hind legs.

205 to 145 million years ago

Jurassic

- Many new types of dinosaurs appeared during this period, including *Allosaurus*, a giant, fearsome meat-eater.
- Birds and bird-like dinosaurs first appeared during this period.

145 to 65 million years ago

Cretaceous

- The Cretaceous period was marked by amazing growth. Flowering plants appeared and modern insects began to buzz.
- Dinosaurs of all different sizes and shapes flourished on Earth.

WHEN Did Birds First Fly?

Some early birds were actually dinosaurs. Researchers say that **millions of years ago**, the dinosaur family split. One branch, which included *Triceratops* and *Stegosaurus*, kept its feet firmly on the ground. The other branch took flight, giving rise to modern birds.

This tiny hummingbird is descended from huge dinosaurs.

Dinosaur fossil showing imprint of feathers

The Birds of Liaoning

Scientists suspected that modern birds evolved from dinosaurs. In 1996, that **speculation** turned to fact. While tilling his orchard in northwest China, Li Yingfang pulled a slab of rock out of the soil. Inside he found the fossil of a strange creature with the skull of a bird. Imprints in the rock suggested the animal had feathers.

Scientists named Li's discovery *Sinosauropteryx*, which means "Chinese lizard wing." It lived around 125 million years ago.

Birds of a Feather

Before *Sinosauropteryx*, people believed animals developed feathers for flight. *Sinosauropteryx* didn't fly. It used its feathers to attract a mate or to defend itself against an attacker. Since Li's discovery, scientists have found other fossils that prove that modern birds evolved from prehistoric dinosaurs, including a distant cousin of the most terrifying **predator** to walk the planet— *Tyrannosaurus rex*.

Caudipteryx, a feathered, peacock-size dinosaur

DID YOU KNOW?

Dinosaurs died off **65 million years ago**, but some of the dino-birds survived. Scientists think their small size might have helped them escape mass **extinction**.

WHEN Do Birds Migrate?

Birds **migrate** from their summer breeding grounds, where they lay their eggs and nurture their young, to their warmer winter homes in search of food and a place to rest. Most of the 650 North American bird species wing their way south every year. Few species stay put throughout the winter.

Why Fly?

Birds that nest in the Northern Hemisphere migrate north in the spring to feast on newly hatching bugs. As winter approaches, the bug population decreases. The birds fly south again.

Not all birds migrate the same distance. Some birds live on sides of mountains and travel from higher to lower elevations. Other birds travel to areas hundreds of miles away. Long-distance migrants usually travel south from Canada and the U.S. to Mexico and South America. They then return in the spring.

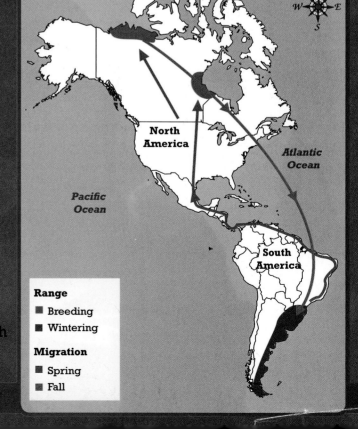

North America

Atlantic Ocean

Pacific Ocean

South America

Range
- Breeding
- Wintering

Migration
- Spring
- Fall

How to Make a Plastic Bottle Bird Feeder

What You Need

- scissors or knife
- eyehook
- 2-liter plastic soda bottle
- string
- 2 twigs or wooden spoons
- birdseed

What to Do

Step 1

Have an adult help you cut a hole in the middle of the soda bottle. Make sure that the hole is large enough to hold the thinnest part of the twig or spoon.

Step 2

Turn the bottle around to cut another hole directly opposite the first hole. This hole should be a little larger than the diameter of a dime.

Step 3

Repeat the first two steps, but this time, place the holes about a quarter of the way up the bottle. Make sure the second hole is a little larger than a dime. After you cut the holes, insert the twigs or the spoons. They will be perches for birds to stand on.

Step 4

Take the cap off of the bottle. Have an adult help you twist a small eyehook into the center of the cap. Next, thread a piece of string through the eyehook and tie a knot to form a loop.

Step 5

Fill the bottle with birdseed. Hang the feeder on a tree branch.

WHEN Did Dogs Become Our Best Friends?

Dogs protect our homes, come when we call them, and lick our faces. How and when did dogs become our best friends?

The Wolf Within

Dogs **evolved** from wolves. Some **14,000 years ago**, perhaps even earlier, humans began to tame these early animals. A few years ago, scientists figured out that all modern dogs descended from Asian wolves.

From Asia with Love

About **6,000 years ago**, dogs in Southeast Asia became isolated from their wolf family. As a result, Asian dogs did not breed with wolves. Instead, dogs walked down their own evolutionary path, developing into our modern-day pets. Scientists suspect that dogs first came to North America about **9,000 years ago**, following early humans across a land bridge that once connected Northern Asia to North America.

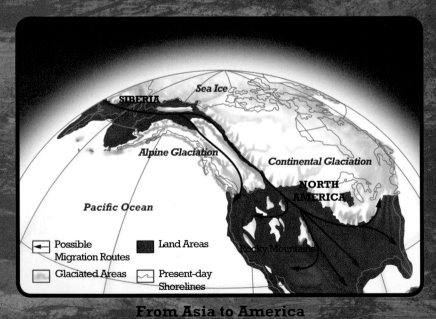

SIBERIA

Sea Ice

Alpine Glaciation

Continental Glaciation

NORTH AMERICA

Pacific Ocean

Rocky Mountains

⬅ Possible Migration Routes

◼ Land Areas

▨ Glaciated Areas

∿ Present-day Shorelines

From Asia to America

TOP 5 Dog Breeds for Pets

	Breed	Ranking 2012
	Labrador Retriever	1
	German Shepherd	2
	Golden Retriever	3
	Beagle	4
	Bulldog	5

Domesticated Dogs

How did dogs become **domesticated**? Some scientists believe the animals tamed themselves, venturing into human campsites to sniff out scraps of food. Dogs that were not afraid of humans ate well, survived, and multiplied. Other scientists think that dogs became tame when humans started to farm and switched to a diet based on grains. Dogs that could digest these grains stayed near the farms, and over time they became suited to a domesticated lifestyle. Still other scientists think humans tamed dogs by capturing and breeding the animals, selecting for certain traits.

WHEN Did the First Domestic Cats Appear?

Like dogs, cats were once wild. Some scientists estimate that cats first became domesticated some 12,000 years ago.

Cat of the Woods

Some scientists believe that cats descended from *Felis sylvestris*, a wildcat that lived in the Middle East. *Felis sylvestris* means "cat of the woods."

A Mouser Hunt

How did cats become tame? Once people began to settle down, cats grew more mild-tempered. Why? Because of something essential to all living things: food. Humans had to store surplus crops during the off-season, and mice invaded these stores of grain. Cats came on the heels of these rodents. Cats got rid of the mice. So humans loved the cats.

Feline Fascination

Ancient Egyptians revered cats, showing them respect by turning them into mummies when the animals died. The ancient Romans saw cats as a symbol of freedom and liberty.

But in the **Middle Ages**, Europeans began to associate cats with witches and evil and began to kill them. Between 1347 and 1353, the **bubonic plague** struck Europe, and millions of people died from the disease. Europe was infested with rats. Fleas on these rats spread the plague. What could stop the spread of rats? Cats. Eventually, cats made a comeback.

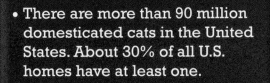

FUN FACTS

- There are more than 90 million domesticated cats in the United States. About 30% of all U.S. homes have at least one.

- A cat's tongue has tiny, backward-facing spines, which make the tongue rough and help the cat clean itself.

- There are about 40 breeds of domestic cats, from long-haired to short-haired.

WHEN Did the First Zoo Open?

In 2009, scientists found an Egyptian animal cemetery that contained the bones of 10 dogs, a baby hippo, and other animals. The site, in the ancient city of Hierakonpolis, is 5,500 years old. Researchers say that the city's rulers kept the animals captive.

The Queen's Menagerie

One of the most famous zoos in ancient history opened in Egypt in 1500 B.C. The zoo was built by Queen Hatshepsut, who collected animals from all over Africa. The oldest zoo in Europe is in Vienna, Austria. It was built by Emperor Franz Josef in 1752, as a gift to his wife.

Queen Hatshepsut's zoo included baboons that had been captured in current-day Somalia.

Philadelphia Zoo

The oldest zoo in the U.S. is the Philadelphia Zoo, in Pennsylvania. It was chartered, or officially registered, in 1859. When it actually opened, in 1874, 3,000 people visited. Admission cost 25 cents for adults and 10 cents for children. The zoo had its own dock so people traveling by steamboat on the Schuylkill River could visit. During its first year, 228,000 people visited the Philadelphia Zoo to see its 813 animals. Today, the zoo is home to 1,300 animals.

People Who Rocked the World

Theodore Roosevelt

Teddy Roosevelt (1858–1919) had many jobs and many interests. He was a writer, a soldier, and, of course, president of the U.S. He was also one of the most highly respected naturalists of his day. As a child, Roosevelt collected all types of animals. He even paid other children to collect things for him. As the 26th president of the U.S., Roosevelt created five national parks, 51 bird sanctuaries, and 18 national monuments, including the Grand Canyon.

WHEN Did People First Talk?

Before there were texts, e-mails, and tweets, there was good old-fashioned talking. Before that, there was silence.

What Is Language?

Dolphins squeak, click, whistle, and squawk. Honeybees dance to let other bees know where to find pollen. Birds sing. Dogs bark. These animals can communicate. But humans are the only social animals that have developed a complex spoken language.

Language is a shared, organized system of sounds, words, and sentences. People use language to communicate what they are thinking. Language also allows people to pass down their history and culture to the next generation.

First Words

It's hard to say when humans first developed a spoken language, but most scholars agree it was about **150,000 years ago**. Some historians suspect humans began talking nonstop some **40,000 years ago**, when the first artistic cave paintings and musical instruments came on the scene.

This cave painting was created about 15,000 years ago in Lascaux, France. It was discovered in 1940.

Say Again?

¿Habla usted español? Parlez-vous français? Sprechen Sie Deutsch? Do you recognize these phrases in Spanish, French, and German? There are about 6,900 languages in the world. Languages spread when people move from place to place. As people settle in their new homes, they take their language with them.

Half of the world's languages will be extinct by 2115. One reason for this is that fewer young people are learning native languages from their parents. Then, when they become parents, they are not able to teach the language to their own children.

WHEN **Did** People Start Using Written Language?

Although people learned how to communicate verbally tens of thousands of years ago, written language emerged much later. The Sumerians, one of the first civilizations that lived in Mesopotamia, developed a written language by about 3100 B.C.

Pictograms

The Sumerians drew simple pictures called pictograms, which symbolized a word or an idea. Sumerian writers pressed the symbols into soft, wet clay tablets using a triangular reed called a stylus. Because the pictures were hard to create, Sumerian **scribes** reduced the pictograms to a series of wedge-shaped characters called cuneiform.

This clay tablet with cuneiform script reveals a count of donkeys and carts.

FUN FACTS

قِف
STOP

- Unlike English, which has 21 consonants and five vowels in its alphabet, the Arabic alphabet has 25 consonants and three vowels.

- Hebrew is read right to left, while English is read left to right.

Writing in Egypt

The ancient Egyptians loved to keep records. Around 6,000 years ago, they invented a system of hieroglyphic writing that represented sounds, just like the alphabet we use today. The Egyptians wrote their hieroglyphs on an early form of paper called papyrus. They also carved them on walls and statues. The Egyptians used about 700 different hieroglyphs.

Ancient Egyptian hieroglyphs

Jean-François Champollion

The Rosetta Stone

For thousands of years, no one could understand Egyptian hieroglyphs. As a result, no one knew the history of ancient Egypt. Then in 1799, a French soldier stumbled on a black rock near Rosetta, Egypt. The rock contained fragments of three different written languages: Greek, Egyptian hieroglyphics, and Egyptian demotic. Experts soon realized the passages were identical. French Egyptologist Jean-François Champollion translated the stone and **deciphered** the hieroglyphs. The Rosetta stone opened the door to understanding Egyptian culture.

The Rosetta stone

WHEN Was the First Book Printed?

Books have been around for centuries. The one you're reading now was created by humans on super-fast computers, but it didn't always work that way.

Before the **mid-1400s**, people printed books by hand. A scribe dipped a **quill** into an inkwell and then wrote a word or two on a blank piece of **parchment**. When the ink on the quill dried, the scribe repeated the process again and again, day after day, year after year. It took a lot of work to copy a book, and usually scribes could only work during daylight hours. That's why books used to be rare and expensive. The Gutenberg Bible (also known as the 42-line Bible, the Mazarin Bible, or the B42) was the first major book printed.

Gutenberg Bible, 1455

A Revolution

In **1440**, German inventor Johannes Gutenberg invented the printing press. The first book ever printed was the Gutenberg Bible in **1455**.

It was a true turning point in history. Because people finally had access to books, it helped them learn to read. News and ideas could travel faster and farther than ever before. It didn't take long for those ideas, spread through pamphlets, newspapers, and books, to start revolutions, as people tried to better their lives and change the structure of their governments.

DID YOU KNOW?

Just 50 years after Gutenberg printed his first page, there were more than 9 million printed books in circulation.

TRY IT!

Gutenberg's press used raised letters. Create your own raised letters using a potato.

What You Will Need

- Potato
- Vegetable brush
- Carving knife ⚠
- Colored marker (fine point)
- Black paint
- Thin aluminum tray
- Several sheets of white paper

Step 1

Scrub a good-sized potato with the vegetable brush until it is clean. With an adult's help, cut the potato in half.

Step 2

Using the marker, draw a symbol or a shape such as an oval on the white part of the potato.

Step 3

With an adult's help, carve the shape from the potato. Slice the edges so that the raised shape stands out.

⚠ Never use a knife without adult supervision!

Step 4

Pour black paint into the aluminum tray. Dip the part of potato with the carved shape into the paint. Let some of the paint drip off. Press the potato against the paper and watch the image appear.

WHEN Was the First Telegraph Sent?

As hard as it is to believe in our high-tech electronic world, it once took weeks or months for people to communicate across long distances. Then Samuel F.B. Morse invented the telegraph, a device that sent electronic signals over wires. Using his system, communication became nearly instant. Morse sent the first telegraph message on May 24, 1844, from the Supreme Court chambers in Washington, D.C., to the B&O Railroad Depot in Baltimore, Maryland.

FUN FACTS

Long before Samuel Morse was a famous inventor, he was an artist. He studied at the Royal Academy of Arts in London. It was hard for Morse to make a living as an artist, though. When he was 41, Morse became an inventor.

How Did It Work?

Morse powered his telegraph using electricity from a battery. The communication itself was carried over an electric wire. Morse turned "on" the electricity at one end of the wire by tapping a send key. When he released the key, Morse turned "off" the electrical current. A receiver was connected to the other end of the wire. The receiver had a small spring that held a strip of iron away from an **electromagnet**. When an electronic dot or dash was sent, the magnet picked up a strip of iron, which produced a sharp click. *Voilà*—a conversation.

Real Time

Morse's telegraph used electronic signals, a series of dots (short signals) and dashes (long signals). Using his code, called Morse Code, a telegraph **operator** could tap a transmitting key at one end of the line while another operator listened at the other end to decode the message.

MORSE CODE

TRY IT!

Using the code shown on this page, write a short note to a friend. Is he or she able to decode it?

WHEN Was the First Successful Telephone Call?

Alexander Graham Bell believed there had to be a different, better way to communicate across distances. He invented a machine that used electricity to transmit human voices over a wire. He called it the "electrical speech machine." We call it the telephone.

"Mr. Watson, come here!"

On **March 10, 1876**, Bell sat in his workshop and fiddled with his invention. When he was ready, he told his assistant, Thomas Watson, to go into another room. Bell spoke into the mouthpiece: "Mr. Watson, come here! I want to see you." When Watson heard Bell, he came running, excited that Bell's "electrical speech machine" actually worked.

Alexander Graham Bell makes the first telephone call between New York and Chicago, 1876.

A Toy?

Most people thought Bell's telephone was interesting, but nothing more than a toy. Bell knew better. He told his father that he could foresee the day when "friends converse with each other without leaving home." By 1905, there were more than 2 million phones in the United States. While the design and technology have changed, the purpose remains basically the same.

1907

1934

1982

1919

1954

2014

A Look Back

The first telephone was big, but simple. Its heart was a microphone that changed the sound waves of a person's voice into electrical signals. Those electrical signals traveled instantly across wires. Inside Bell's "electrical speech machine" was a loudspeaker that reproduced every syllable a person uttered.

A Look Forward

The same basic technology that allows you to call a friend on your cell phone hasn't changed much since Bell called out for Watson. Like Bell's telephone, a cell phone still uses electricity supplied by a battery, microphone, and loudspeaker. However, cell phones do not use wires to transmit electrical signals. Instead, cell phones send and receive radio signals.

WHEN **Did** Radio First Use Broadcast Signals?

Long before TVs, MP3s, and iPods, there were radios. On December 12, 1901, an Italian inventor named Guglielmo Marconi sent the first wireless radio transmission, or broadcast. It traveled across the Atlantic Ocean from Cornwall, England, to St. John's, Newfoundland, Canada, a distance of about 2,100 miles (3,379 kilometers). The accomplishment landed Marconi in history books. He was just 24 years old.

DIY Guy

As a boy, Marconi spent hours studying science books. As a young man, he performed experiments with wires and batteries. He studied electricity with Heinrich Hertz, who discovered **radio waves**. Marconi thought it was possible to use these invisible waves to communicate.

Oh, Canada

In 1897, Marconi telegraphed a message across a distance of about 12 miles (19 km) using Morse Code. Next, he tackled the Atlantic Ocean. Marconi built a high-powered transmission station in Cornwall, England, and a receiving station in St. John's, Newfoundland, Canada. The Canadian station included a massive **antenna** held aloft by balloons. Although some believed Marconi's experiment would fail, the broadcast was a success.

All the Ships at Sea

Soon, people could communicate across continents and ships at sea could correspond with people on land. Eventually, people used radios to speak directly to each other. Modern-day radios look nothing like their predecessors.

FUN FACTS

- Radio waves travel through the air at the speed of light—186,282 miles (299,792 km) per second.

- More than 90% of Americans listen to the radio each day, for an average of about 92 minutes.

1930 ▶ **1960** ▶ **2000** ▶ **2014**

WHEN Was the TV Invented?

Some people love watching television, and some people hate it. However, most people cannot imagine life without it. Almost all American homes have at least one television, and many homes have three or four. Imagine what life was like before television. It was not that long ago.

Television was invented in the 1920s.

Compared to today's big screens, TV sets of the 1930s were tiny.

The Development of Television

Although some sets were available as early as the 1930s, most Americans did not see a television show before 1945. By the end of the 1950s, televisions were in about 90% of American homes, and in the 1950s, colored TV sets also became available. The first television programs in color were broadcast in 1951.

TV Through the Years

1940s   1950s   1960s   1970s

A Look Back

In **1946**, a 10-inch television cost $352 (about $3,100 in 2013 dollars).

A Look Forward

In **2013**, Samsung produced the S9, an ultra high definition 85-inch television set that cost $40,000.

Historic Events

Television connects the world. Many people remember the moment they were watching television when they learned of an important event. Do you?

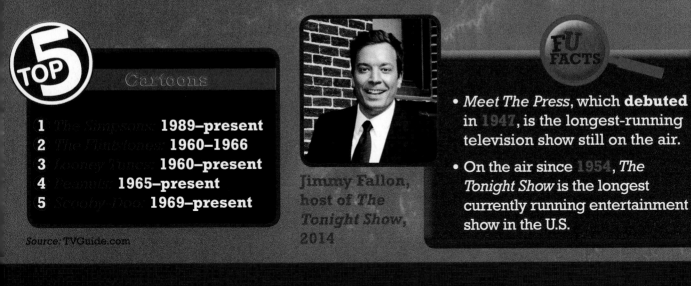

TOP 5 — Cartoons

1	The Simpsons:	**1989–present**
2	The Flintstones:	**1960–1966**
3	Looney Tunes:	**1960–present**
4	Peanuts:	**1965–present**
5	Scooby-Doo:	**1969–present**

Source: TVGuide.com

Jimmy Fallon, host of *The Tonight Show*, 2014

FUN FACTS

- *Meet The Press*, which **debuted** in 1947, is the longest-running television show still on the air.
- On the air since 1954, *The Tonight Show* is the longest currently running entertainment show in the U.S.

1980s   1990s   2000s   2010s

WHEN Did the Internet Begin?

People access the Internet on computers, smartphones, tablets, and other devices. You can browse anywhere, even on airplanes, to gain immediate access to all sorts of information, from sports scores to breaking news.

From ARPANET to the Internet

No one person invented the Internet. The idea took root in the 1960s, when the U.S. government set out to develop a special communications system called ARPANET. A few years later, colleges and universities started their own computer **networks** to virtually share information.

World Wide Browsing

In 1989, a British scientist named Tim Berners-Lee made the Internet accessible by inventing **hypertext transfer protocol**, or http. In short, Berners-Lee built the first Web browser. Because of hypertext, we can view text and pictures on our computers or mobile devices. It links computer systems across the globe.

Bill Gates

In the past, people used difficult commands to access information on computers. It was tough going—complicated keystrokes and procedures to complete simple tasks. Bill Gates imagined a better way. He invented Windows, which allows PC users to click through screens, or "windows." His successful software company, called Microsoft, made Gates one of the richest people in the world.

Bill Gates, pictured in 1986 at Microsoft

WHEN Did Communication Expand?

From the first cave paintings to the latest mobile technology, humans are always trying to make communication better and easier. Here are some other communication milestones worth buzzing about.

1045

First Movable Type

In 1045, a Chinese printer named Bi Sheng invented the first movable type. At first, Sheng carved Chinese characters into wood and placed them on an iron board, which he then pressed onto paper. He eventually made the movable characters from clay.

Hold the Presses

In the 1600s, the first modern newspapers hit newsstands in Venice, Italy. The ancient Romans are credited with printing the first newspaper, or daily public records, called the *Acta Diurna*, sometime around 59 B.C.

1960

Balloon Science

NASA launched the world's first communications satellite on August 12, 1960. Named *Echo 1*, the balloon-shaped satellite orbited 1,000 miles (1,609 km) above Earth. The satellite made it possible to communicate instantaneously.

Was the First Hot-Air Balloon Launched?

Joseph Montgolfier always wondered why smoke rose into the air. He wondered if he could use whatever "force" was causing the smoke to rise to create some kind of flying machine. Working with his brother, Jacques-Etienne, Joseph hit on an idea: the hot-air balloon.

On September 19, 1783, Joseph and Etienne made history above the skies of Versailles, France. The king and queen were on hand to watch as the balloon took flight. It floated for about eight minutes and landed two miles away. The brothers didn't actually ride in the balloon's basket. Instead, the passengers were their pets: a duck, a sheep, and a rooster.

Full of Hot Air

What exactly caused the Montgolfier balloon to rise? Simple—hot air. Warm air is lighter than cold air, which means warm air has less mass per unit of volume than cold air. Hot air rises above cold air. If you heat air by 100 degrees, it loses about a quarter of its weight. The more hot air there is inside a balloon, the more weight it can lift.

Montgolfier balloon

Up, Up, and Away

The first balloons were full of hot air, but that changed over time. Gases such as helium and hydrogen can also make a balloon soar.

1783

Joseph and Etienne Montgolfier launch the first small hot-air balloon on **June 4, 1783,** over the village of Annonay, France.

J.F. Pilâtre de Rozier and François Laurent become the first humans to fly. The pair drift over Paris on **November 21, 1783,** for about 20 minutes in a hot-air balloon designed by the Montgolfier brothers.

1785

A French balloonist, Jean-Pierre Blanchard, along with an American copilot, John Jeffries, become the first people to cross the English Channel in a hot-air balloon.

1892

The first weather balloons are built in France. The balloons carry instruments that measure barometric pressure, temperature, and humidity.

1907

Anderson Rubber Company in Akron, Ohio, makes the first hot-air balloons in the United States.

1982

An American truck driver named Larry Walters filled 45 weather balloons with helium. He hooked the balloons to a lawn chair and lifted off from his backyard in San Pedro, California. The ride took Walters more than 15,000 feet (4,572 meters) into the air.

1996

Balloonist Steve Fossett successfully crosses the Pacific Ocean flying **solo** in a helium balloon. He traveled from Korea to Canada in four days.

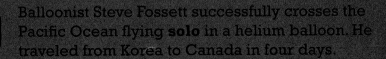

Was the first Mechanical Flight?

On _____, Orville Wright became the first human to take to the air in a mechanical airplane. The first flight occurred at Kitty Hawk, a windswept island in North Carolina. The plane traveled 120 feet (36.58 m). Though the flight lasted only 12 seconds, it gave a glimpse of the future of air travel.

Working Hard

The Wright brothers worked diligently to defy **gravity**. They studied every article and book they could find about **aeronautics**. They built **gliders** and studied the principles of **balance**, **lift**, and **control**. The brothers made three more flights that December day. The longest was 852 feet (260 m). Afterward, Orville sent his father a telegraph: *"Success…Four flights…Longest 57 seconds…Inform press. Home for Christmas."*

Wilbur and Orville Wright

DID YOU KNOW?

Some people claim that Gustave Whitehead, not Orville Wright, was the first human to fly in a mechanical airplane. Whitehead's flight allegedly occurred more than two years before the Wright brothers flew their plane at Kitty Hawk. Apparently, Whitehead's flying machine, the *Condor*, took off from Bridgeport, Connecticut, on August 14, 1901, and flew 50 feet (15.24 m) into the air.

Did the German-born aviator actually take the world's first flight? In 2013, an international aviation magazine called *Jane's All the World's Aircraft* recognized Whitehead's achievement. But the title of being first in flight is still up in the air.

The Wright *Flyer*

WHEN did the First Commercial Airliner Take Off?

On January 1, 1914, Antony H. Jannus sat behind the controls of an airboat owned by the St. Petersburg-Tampa Airboat Line. He fired up the engines and took off across Tampa Bay in Florida. It was the world's first winged airliner and the world's first airline flight.

DID YOU KNOW?

The first prepacked in-flight meal was served on October 11, 1919, during a flight from London to Paris.

Cloth and Wire

This plane was built with wood, cloth, and wire. On board was Abram C. Pheil, the first-ever airline passenger. He sat on a small wooden seat near the pilot and wore a raincoat so he would not get wet.

Jannus unexpectedly had to land in the water to fix the sputtering engine. He took off again and landed safely on the Hillsborough River. A crowd of 3,500 people greeted Jannus and Pheil.

FUN FACTS

The regular price of the ticket was $5 for the 22-minute trip from St. Petersburg to Tampa. But Pheil paid $400 for his ticket, which was sold at auction to the highest bidder.

WHEN Was the First Nonstop Solo Transatlantic Flight?

At 7:52 a.m. on May 20, 1927, a little-known airmail pilot named Charles Lindbergh flew into history. Taking off from Roosevelt Field on Long Island, New York, Lindbergh spent 33 hours and 30 minutes flying alone through fog and sleet across the Atlantic Ocean. It was the first time anyone had ever accomplished such a feat. When his plane, the *Spirit of St. Louis*, touched down at Le Bourget Field in Paris, France, 150,000 people were waiting to honor him. Lindbergh became an international superstar.

Lindy Who?

Before his flight across the Atlantic, Lindbergh was just one of many pilots who flew letters and packages from town to town. Lindbergh thought it would be a great idea to cross the Atlantic alone. He carefully planned every step of his trip and stripped down the *Spirit of St. Louis* to make it light and able to be filled with a lot of fuel.

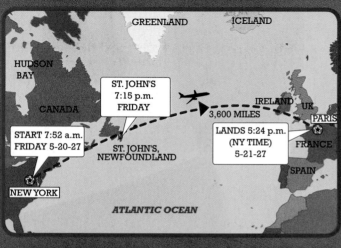

Lindbergh's transatlantic flight

Fly Boys

Lindbergh was first to fly solo across the Atlantic. But before him, two British flyers, John Alcock and Arthur Brown, flew together nonstop across the Atlantic. In 1919, with Alcock at the controls, the pair left Newfoundland, Canada, and ultimately landed in County Galway in Ireland, a 1,864-mile (3,000 kilometer) trip.

People Who Rocked the World

Amelia Earhart

When Amelia Earhart saw her first plane at age 10, she was not all that impressed. It wasn't until 10 years later that she fell in love with aviation. She learned to fly and competed in an air derby for women, nicknamed the "Powder Puff Derby." In May 1932, five years after Lindbergh's flight, Earhart became the first female pilot to fly nonstop across the Atlantic. Earhart flew more than 2,000 miles (3,219 km) from Newfoundland, Canada, to Ireland. The trip set a new record of 14 hours, 56 minutes.

Earhart went on to break many more aviation records. She was the first person, man or woman, to fly across the Pacific Ocean from Hawaii to California. In 1937, Earhart tried to become the first woman to fly around the world. Tragically, her plane vanished over the Pacific. The U.S. Navy searched for Earhart and navigator Frederick J. Noonan, but they were never found.

WHEN Did the
Hindenburg Explode?

The *Hindenburg*, with its 61 crew members and 36 passengers, left Germany on **May 3**. It traveled over the Atlantic Ocean, battling headwinds that delayed its arrival. Zeppelins didn't land like airplanes—they had to be fastened to huge towers.

The Last Flight

On **May 6, 1937**, the residents of Lakehurst, New Jersey, were treated to a view of a zeppelin called the *Hindenburg*. For 30 years, passengers had been traveling on these huge, **hydrogen**-filled luxury airships. But as the *Hindenburg* was about to touch down at a U.S. Naval air station, it exploded into a raging ball of fire, causing one of the greatest air disasters in history.

What Caused the Explosion?

A few minutes after the landing lines were lowered, a fire broke out. The hydrogen inside the ship ignited and exploded. Thirty-five people on board the airship died that day, as did one person on the ground.

Anatomy of a Zeppelin

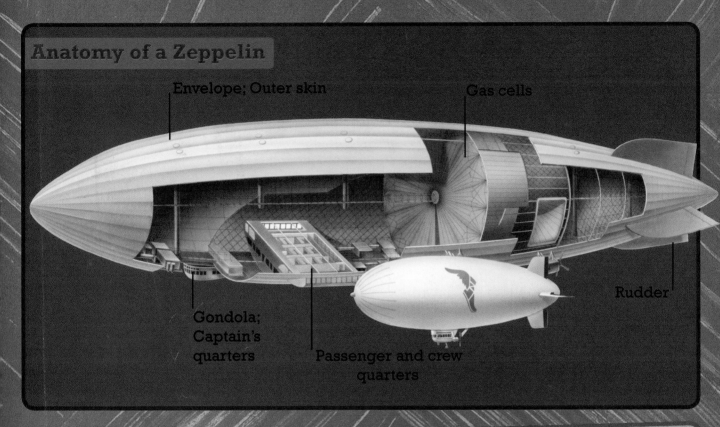

Envelope; Outer skin

Gas cells

Gondola; Captain's quarters

Passenger and crew quarters

Rudder

The *Hindenburg* at a Glance

- **Length:** 803.8 feet (245 m)
- **Diameter:** 135.1 feet (41 m)
- **Cruising speed:** 78 miles per hour (126 km per hour)
- **Maximum speed:** 84 miles per hour (135 km per hour)

WHEN Did an Airplane First Break the Sound Barrier?

If you were in the Mojave Desert in California on October 14, 1947, you might have thought a thunderstorm was approaching. An ear-shattering roar thundered across the sky. The sound was a sonic boom, the telltale noise made when an airplane travels faster than the speed of sound.

Glennis Goes Glam

On that day, U.S. Air Force pilot Chuck Yeager, flying in an **experimental** jet, "pushed the envelope" to break the sound barrier. Yeager nicknamed the plane the *Glamorous Glennis*, after his wife.

Before Yeager's flight, no airplane had traveled faster than sound, roughly 760 miles per hour (1,223 km per hour) at sea level. Other pilots attempted it, but their planes often broke apart as they got closer to their goal.

Yeager's flight was dangerous. Aircrews attached the X-1 jet to a B-29 bomber. The bomber flew high above the desert and dropped Yeager's plane. As the plane approached the speed of sound, its controls locked up. But Yeager remained calm and in control. Soon, officials on the ground heard the deafening *boom* as the sound barrier was shattered.

Waves on the Roll

Sound is a form of energy created when objects, such as air **molecules**, vibrate. The X-1 moved so fast that it pushed those molecules ahead of it like a snowplow. Usually, when a plane moves through the air, sound waves move ahead of the plane. But when a plane breaks the sound barrier, sound waves are squeezed together into a shock wave—a loud sonic boom.

**U.S. Air Force SR-71
Blackbird spy plane**

A Look Back

The first jet airplane took flight on **August 27, 1939**, high above Germany, although the Germans did not come up with the idea. That distinction goes to an Englishman named Frank Whittle, a British Royal Air Force **engineer** on a mission to move airplanes beyond propellers.

A Look Forward

One experimental plane, the Solar Flapper, does what its name implies: flaps its wings. NASA's concept plane, illustrated below, could one day be real. Scientists hope to build an aircraft that uses solar power to flap its wings and soar through the air.

WHEN Did a Human First Travel into Space?

On April 12, 1961, Russian cosmonaut Yuri Gagarin became the first person to travel to space. Gagarin's mission lasted only 108 minutes. After breaking free of Earth's gravity, the round space capsule made one orbit and then landed safely back on Soviet soil. The Soviet Air Force pilot was only 27 years old.

Yuri Gagarin

The Space Race

After Gagarin's flight, the U.S. government hurried to build an aircraft that could successfully send a human into orbit. On May 5, 1961, astronaut Alan Shepard became the first American in space. In 1962, John Glenn became the first U.S. astronaut to circle the Earth.

Alan Shepard

John Glenn

Soviet astronauts are called cosmonauts. The first female in space was Valentina Vladimirovna Tereshkova. She circled Earth 48 times in 1963.

TRY IT!

Try this simple activity so you can understand how a rocket works.

What You Will Need

- Cork
- Nail
- Air pump and needle
- Empty plastic soda bottle (any size)
- Water
- 16-inch cinder block or some other stable surface

What to Do

Step 1

If the cork is long, cut it in half so that you have pieces of equal length. Use the nail to punch a hole through the cork's center. Push the air pump needle all the way through the hole.

Step 2

Fill the soda bottle a quarter of the way with water. Plug the bottle with the cork. Make sure it is a tight fit. Hook the air pump up to the needle.

Step 3

With the help of an adult, stand the bottle with the cork end down against the side of a cinder block. Angle the bottle away from the two of you. Next, have an adult pump air into the bottle. Watch your bottle rocket blast off!

WHEN Did a Spacecraft First Land on Mars?

On **December 2, 1971,** the former Soviet Union beat the U.S. in the space race to Mars. On that date, a Soviet-built Martian **probe** called Mars 3 landed on the Red Planet. The Mars 3 mission consisted of a lander and a satellite that orbited the planet. The lander carried a small rover that was supposed to explore the surface of Mars.

The success of the mission was short-lived, however. Some 14 seconds after touchdown, the Mars 3 lander stopped communicating with Earth. Before communications failed, the lander sent a blurry image back to Earth. It was the first photo from the Martian surface.

Mars rover

Viking Power

On July 20, 1976, an unmanned American spacecraft called *Viking* became the first spacecraft to land on Mars. It was the first of two NASA *Viking* probes. Both *Vikings* made amazing discoveries as they studied the Martian soil and atmosphere.

Search for Life

The main goal of the *Viking* probes was to discover whether life existed on the Red Planet. In one experiment, the probes scooped up soil and mixed it with a drop of water that contained nutrients. If the Martian soil contained microbes, which are tiny living organisms, the soil would react with the nutrients in the water. The soil would then release radioactive carbon dioxide or methane, a gas that living organisms expel. The initial findings were exciting. Some scientists thought that the experiment showed that life did indeed exist on Mars.

But other experiments did not back up the findings. Scientists debated the matter for years. In 2012, NASA experts reviewed the original data. They now believe that the earlier *Viking* experiments may have found evidence of life.

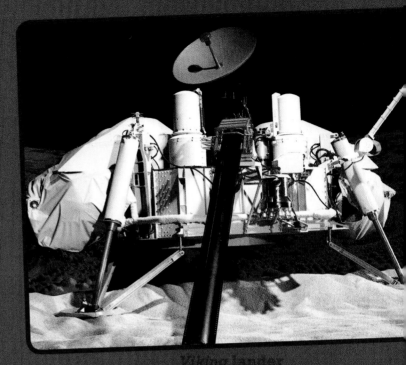

Viking lander

Science Fiction or Fact?

Mars has always been a hot topic for writers, artists, and moviemakers. In 1898, H.G. Wells created a Martian invasion story in *The War of the Worlds*. Years later, Ray Bradbury wrote *The Martian Chronicles*, which tells a tale of how humans colonized Mars as the Martian race disappeared.

Hollywood has made dozens of movies about the planet, some silly and some serious. In one, called *Santa Claus Conquers the Martians*, Martians kidnap Santa because there is nobody on Mars to give presents to Martian children.

WHEN Did Humans First Walk on the Moon?

On July 20, 1969, U.S. astronaut Neil Armstrong became the first human to walk on the moon. "That's one small step for man, one giant leap for mankind," Armstrong said as he put the first footprint on the lunar surface in a spot called the Sea of Tranquility. The time was 10:56 p.m. in New York City.

Armstrong, along with astronauts Edwin "Buzz" Aldrin Jr. and Michael Collins, had traveled 240,000 miles (386,243 km) aboard *Apollo 11*. They blasted off from the Kennedy Space Center in Florida on July 16, 1969. The lunar landing marked the end of the space race between the U.S. and the Soviet Union. By 1972, the U.S. had sent five more successful manned missions to the moon.

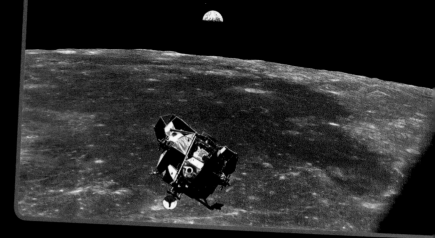

Missions to the Moon

Although the *Apollo 11* mission was the first time humans had landed on the moon, it was not the first time humans had visited it. In December 1968, the astronauts of *Apollo 8* became the first humans to travel to the moon. Frank Borman, James Lovell Jr., and William Anders also became the first humans to see the dark side of the moon.

A Look Back

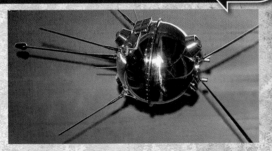

In **1959**, the Soviet Union crash-landed an unmanned probe onto the moon's surface. It was the first time a human-built object reached the lunar surface. The U.S. responded by shifting its own space program into high gear. The Soviets never landed a person on the moon.

A Look Forward

Should humans build permanent bases on the moon? In **2011**, U.S. lawmakers introduced a bill in Congress to return humans to the moon by **2022** with the goal of building a permanent settlement. The last time humans walked on the moon was **1972**.

WHEN **Did** People Start Cooking with Fire?

Many things make humans human. We communicate through language, we walk upright, and we have thumbs, a feature that makes our lives much easier. We also cook our food with fire, a big upgrade in lifestyle and a huge development. No one knows, however, exactly when humans first started cooking with fire.

Cooking with *Homo erectus*

Richard Wrangham, an anthropologist at Harvard University, believes that an early human called *Homo erectus* used fire to cook some 1.8 million years ago. Compared to earlier hominids, *Homo erectus* had a smaller jaw and teeth, yet had a larger brain. These distinctive traits, according to Wrangham, could only come about if *Homo erectus* was eating softer food—food that had been cooked.

Lunch with the Neanderthals

Archaeologist Wil Roebroeks says that *Neanderthals* started cooking with fire some 300,000 to 400,000 years ago. Roebroeks argues that there is no evidence of humans cooking with fire before that time.

Chef of the Past

Scientist Dennis Sandgathe says that modern humans did not cook with fire until just 12,000 years ago. In historical terms, this is a mere tick of the evolutionary clock.

Why Can't Scientists Agree?

When looking at ancient campsites, it is tough to figure out what caused a fire. It could have been an accident like a lightning strike or a volcano, or an **intentional** act like somebody rubbing two sticks together.

Humans Over Time

The study of human ancestry is tricky business. Though scientists have learned a lot about our history, exact dates are hard to pin down. Here's an approximate look at where we came from.

4.4 million years ago

Ardipithecus ramidus: The earliest human (whose bones were ever found) walked on two legs and lived in the forest.

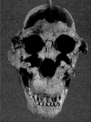

3.85–2.95 million years ago

Australopithecus afarensis: Studies of their teeth show that this species ate many different kinds of food. Some grew to be five feet tall.

2.4–1.4 million years ago

Homo habilis: Known as "handy man," this early human was the first to use **primitive** tools.

1.89 million–143,000 years ago

Homo erectus: This early human species was very similar to modern humans.

200,000–28,000 years ago

Homo neanderthalensis: Neanderthals had short limbs and sloping foreheads. Recent studies have revealed that Neanderthals were relatively intelligent and evolved.

100,000 years ago–present

Homo sapiens **(modern humans):** Our species has likely been around for nearly **100,000 years**, though some scientists say that figure is closer to **200,000 years**.

WHEN Did People Begin Using Water as a Source of Power?

Have you ever wondered why most people live near bodies of water? Water makes it easy to travel from one place to another, and it's also a source of power. Over the centuries, rushing water has helped people build homes, feed their families, and make clothes. The ability to harness waterpower, which is also known as hydropower, was a critical step in the development of modern civilization.

The Power Wheel

The ancient Greeks ground flour by hand. Around 2,100 years ago, someone realized that water could do some of the work. The result was the waterwheel. The power of rushing water turned a wheel, which turned a **grindstone** that ground grain into flour. The Greeks and others then applied the technology to textile making, woodworking, and more.

Wooden wheel of an ancient water mill in an open-air museum, Czech Republic

Turning on the Lights

Rushing water can power more than a grindstone—it can electrify a lightbulb or power a factory. It's known as hydroelectric power. Dams on rivers convert the energy of rushing water into electricity by using a turbine, a modern version of the ancient waterwheel. The world's largest hydroelectric plant, the Three Gorges Dam in China, uses 26 turbines.

FUN FACTS

- About 20% of the world's electricity comes from hydroelectric power.

- The Three Gorges Dam is 1.4 miles (2.3 km) long and 610 feet (186 m) tall. The dam holds back so much water that it created a huge lake that is about 375 miles (600 km) long. It took 13 years to build the dam, which was completed in 2006.

Three Gorges Dam

Model of the Three Gorges Dam

WHEN Was Electricity Discovered?

Most of you know the story. In 1752, Ben Franklin, in an attempt to prove that electricity and lightning were the same thing, flew a kite with a key tied to a string in a thunderstorm. The kite was hit by lightning, so the story goes, and Franklin felt a shock when the electricity hit the key he was holding. Historians now doubt that this incident ever occurred. What Franklin had discovered was how to make lightning travel through a path of least resistance from the air to the ground. His experiment resulted in the invention of the lightning rod, which minimized the risk of houses catching fire from a lightning strike.

Electrical Feathers

People knew what electricity was long before Franklin was born. An ancient Greek scientist named Thales (624–546 B.C.) recognized and recorded the effects of electricity. Of course, no one called it electricity at the time. Thales rubbed amber, a kind of fossilized hard **resin**, against a piece of wool. During his experiments, bits of grass, straw, and a bird's feathers moved toward the amber and clung to it. The effect that Thales described, using different terms, was static electricity.

What's in a Name

In 1600, William Gilbert first used the term "electricity" to describe how electricity and **magnetism** were related. Gilbert discovered some basic things about electricity that set off a round of discoveries by other scientists.

TRY IT!

Build an Electromagnet

An electromagnet cannot work without electricity. Let's build an electromagnet to see how the two are related.

What You Need

- One 3-foot piece of copper wire
- A 6-volt battery
- A large nail
- Paper clips or staples

What to Do

Step 1

With an adult's help, strip the plastic insulation off both ends of the wire.

Step 2

Next, connect one end of the wire around the positive pole of the battery. Wrap the wire around the nail, and then connect the other end of the wire around the negative pole of the battery.

Step 3

Spread some paper clips or staples on a table. Take hold of the nail, put the end near the paper clips or staples, and watch what happens.

WHEN Were Gas Lamps Invented?

Long before lightbulbs lit up the world, gas lamps **illuminated** people's lives. First used in 1792, gas lamps changed the way people lived and worked. Gas was an inexpensive way to light a building or a street corner, making it possible for people to work longer and making city streets safer. William Murdock, an engineer who was born in Scotland, invented the gas lamp.

Burning the Candle

Before gas lamps, people used candles and lamps fueled by oils from whales, fish, sesame seeds, and other natural substances. Murdock's idea changed all that. The time of using candlelight as the primary way to light up the night quickly passed. Lamplights began springing up all over Great Britain and eventually around the world. Early gas lamps were nothing more than iron caps with holes; a person lit the gas with a match, which created a flame. By 1826, British cities were ablaze in the glow of the gas lamp.

Life-Changing Lamplights

The lamplight was revolutionary. After it was invented, cities never slept. People could safely walk the streets at night and shopkeepers could show off their merchandise after hours. People also began to work longer hours. Even theaters got in on the act, using gaslights as footlights to allow people to watch performances at night.

DID YOU KNOW?

On **February 17, 1817**, Baltimore, Maryland, became the first city in the United States to be lit by gas lamps.

WHEN Was the First Oil Well Drilled?

On August 27, 1859, the world's first oil well was drilled in Titusville, a tiny town in western Pennsylvania. After trying for more than a year, drillers struck a pool of oil some 69 feet (21 m) deep. The excitement of that first well sparked the modern oil industry.

Before that momentous day, people like George Bissell waited for oil to seep up through cracks in the earth. Collecting the "rock oil" was a hard way to make a living until Edwin L. Drake came along. Drake believed that there had to be a better way to extract oil from the ground. He was right.

Edwin Drake

The Drake Well

Drake became part owner in Bissell's company, the Pennsylvania Rock Oil Company. He convinced Bissell to drill for oil, instead of collecting oil that had seeped up onto the ground. A year-and-a-half later, in 1859, the first oil gusher began spewing thick, black **crude** oil. The strike made Bissell very rich. Drake, on the other hand, didn't have a head for business and died a poor man.

Texas-Size Strike

For centuries, Native Americans had known that Texas was oil-rich. They could see black crude seeping from the ground. Many used the oil tar as medicine.

On January 10, 1901, an oil well on a salt mound called Spindletop Hill exploded with an enormous **geyser** of thick, black crude that shot 150 feet (46 m) into the air. The oil spewed for nine days before workers could cap the well. Within weeks, more than 40,000 oil workers poured into the region. Many of today's major oil companies, including Gulf, Texaco, and Exxon, can trace their roots to this tiny hill.

Crude Oil Uses

1 Gasoline
2 Heating oil
3 Diesel fuel
4 Jet fuel
5 Kerosene

Oil gushing from Spindletop Hill in Beaumont, Texas

WHEN Does a Solar Cell Generate Electricity?

Solar cells use the sun's power to generate electricity. You've seen them on pocket calculators, roofs, and light posts. Large panels of solar cells can provide enough power to heat and cool a building.

Solar energy has its limits. It can't work at night, nor can it work when it's raining or cloudy. To complicate matters further, while some regions get a lot of sun, some places get very little. When solar cells do work, they can convert only 20–24% of the sun's power into electricity.

Flying Photons

Solar cells are also known as photovoltaic cells. These so-called PV cells are made of semiconductors, special materials that conduct electricity. Sunlight is made up of tiny particles of energy called photons. When a photon smacks up against a solar cell, the material in the PV cell absorbs the photon's energy and turns it into electricity. That electricity is then stored in batteries.

Using the sun as a source of power is not a new concept. The ancient Greek scientist Archimedes supposedly used a bronze shield to focus sunlight onto a wooden ship, sending the ship up in flames. In the **1830s**, British astronomer John Herschel built a solar oven. He used it to cook food during a trip to Africa.

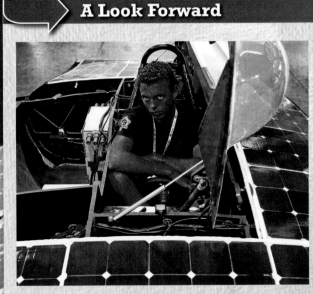

Solar cells might one day power all automobiles. They already power some race cars. Every two years, college students participate in the American Solar Challenge, a cross-country race of solar cars. The racers travel up to 1,800 miles (2,897 km) over a period of several days. The team with the shortest time wins.

2008

Thanks to its advanced lithium-ion batteries and a rooftop solar panel, the visionary 2008 Fisker Karma hybrid can travel 50 miles on electric power alone. This eco-sports car is capable of going 0–60 mph (0–97 kph) in 5.8 seconds, with a top speed of 125 mph (201 kph). It was on display at the 2008 Detroit Auto Show.

WHEN Did a Nuclear Power Plant First Generate Electricity?

Idaho is known for its potatoes. It is also known for something more electrifying. On December 20, 1951, a **nuclear reactor** began generating electricity in the town of Arco. The reactor was not very big, but it was the first nuclear reaction to power a lightbulb—four, to be exact.

Three years later, in the Russian town of Obninsk, a nuclear power plant called APS 1 went online. It generated five megawatts of electricity and is considered the world's first commercial nuclear power plant. By 2013, there were 437 nuclear power plants in 31 countries, according to the European Nuclear Society.

Atomic Blast

Nuclear power wasn't designed to light up a room or power a refrigerator. Instead, nuclear power was first used as a powerful weapon at the end of World War II **(1939–1945)**. Once the war was over, scientists started to find other uses for this new source of energy.

Zwentendorf nuclear power plant, Austria

Splitting Atoms

Nuclear reactions occur when atoms split, a process known as fission. Fission occurs when a **neutron** from one atom hits the nucleus of another atom. When that happens, atoms release more neutrons that strike other atoms. On and on it goes . . . a chain reaction. As the atoms change, they spit out a huge amount of energy, which is called **radiation**.

People Who Rocked the World

Marie Curie

Marie Curie and her husband Pierre discovered radiation. They discovered that a black rock called pitchblende emitted rays of energy. The Curies found that two unknown elements in the pitchblende were giving off the rays. One element was polonium, the other was radium. Her work earned her the Nobel Prize in Physics in 1903 and in Chemistry in 1911. In 1934, she died of leukemia, a cancer of the blood. Many believe Curie's work with radioactivity caused the disease.

Temelin nuclear power plant, in the Czech Republic, is the country's largest power source.

WHEN Did People Begin Using Wind as a Form of Power?

Whether used to power sailing ships or to pump water from wells, wind has been a source of power for centuries. Nearly **5,500 years ago**, the ancient Egyptians figured out that if they rigged a sail on their boats, they could speed up and down the Nile River. Simple windmills ground grain in Persia and pumped water in ancient China.

Grinding Grain

As the centuries wore on, people began to find new ways to use wind as a source of energy. In the **900s**, people in the Middle East built windmills to grind grain into flour. The Europeans saw how well the windmill worked and brought the invention home with them.

Many Uses for Wind

Around **1180**, Europeans were using mills to grind grain. A couple of centuries later, the Dutch were using windmills to drain swampy fields, and the French used windmills to water their crops. American colonists used windmills to grind wheat and corn and to cut wood at sawmills.

Lights On

In **1888**, American inventor Charles F. Brush figured out how to use the power of the wind to turn a turbine that produced electricity. Brush's windmill was 56 feet in diameter and had 144 blades. Using pulleys and belts, the windmill spun a dynamo, which was connected to 408 batteries in Brush's basement. The batteries could light up 350 lightbulbs.

Today, modern windmills are called wind turbines, and these **21st-century** turbines generate electricity. Wind turbines look like huge airplane propellers on a pole. The wind slams unevenly against the blades, which are shaped like the wing of an airplane. The air pressure created by the wind causes the blades to spin, and a **generator** converts mechanical power into electrical power.

WHEN Will the Sun Stop Burning?

Scientists know that one day the sun will burn itself out. The good news is that this won't happen for at least another 5 to 7 billion years.

Sunrise over Earth

Twinkle, Twinkle Little Sun

The sun is a **gargantuan** ball of super-heated gas. Its mass is roughly 333,000 times greater than the mass of Earth. About a million Earths could fit inside the sun, which generates as much energy every second as all of the power plants on Earth could generate in 2 million years! The sun gets its power through fusion, which joins the **nuclei** of atoms to create a nuclear reaction. Fusion takes place deep inside the sun at extremely high temperatures. During this reaction, hydrogen changes to helium. That's why the sun shines.

Out of Gas

At some point, the sun will run out of gas—hydrogen gas, to be specific. When that happens, the sun will begin burning the helium it has stored for billions of years. Its core will collapse on itself, and the sun's radius will expand to more than 200 times its current size. It will grow so large that it will nearly reach Mars, which is 142 million miles (229 million km) away.

FUN FACTS

Every once in a while, the sun gets dark spots known as sunspots. Sunspots are massive, roughly the size of Earth.

So Long, Sun!

When the sun starts to die, Earth won't be far behind. The ever-expanding sun will dry out Earth's oceans and destroy its atmosphere. Ironically, as Earth dies, the outer planets of our solar system will warm up. Some scientists think this could make these planets **habitable**. Perhaps by then humans will have developed the technology to **colonize** the other planets.

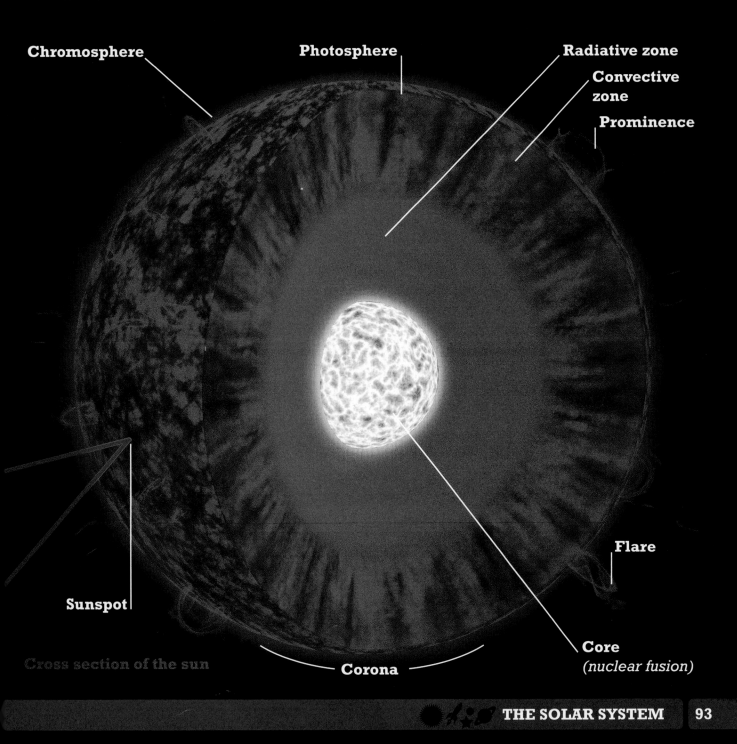

Chromosphere

Photosphere

Radiative zone

Convective zone

Prominence

Flare

Sunspot

Core
(nuclear fusion)

Corona

Cross section of the sun

WHEN Did Life on Earth Begin?

Earth is home to an amazing variety of living things. Some of these creatures are as tiny as bacteria, others are as tall as a redwood tree. Earth is about 4.5 billion years old. As far as we know, it is the only planet in our solar system that supports life. Why is that? Earth is just the right distance from the sun, which means it's a great place for water, oxygen, and the other elements necessary for life as we know it to form and thrive.

Happy Birthday?

Life began forming on Earth some 3.8 billion years ago. But no one really knows exactly how or when. Some scientists believe that Earth's first creatures developed deep in the ocean near openings that gushed warm, **nutrient**-rich water. Others believe meteorites rammed into early Earth, seeding the planet with molecules vital for life.

A meteor striking Earth's atmosphere

Simple Creatures

Earth's first residents were simple one-celled creatures that became more complex over time. Eventually, they evolved into all the plants and animals that exist today. Most plants and animals live in places that aren't too hot or too cold. They need just the right amount of water, sunlight, and oxygen to survive.

Bacteria, shown here, are one of the tiniest forms of life.

YOU DON'T SAY!

Some of Earth's creatures live in extreme conditions. They're called extremophiles. Some live deep in the ocean where it is very dark and cold. Others live in **acidic** waters that would kill other forms of life. By studying these strange creatures, scientists have gained an understanding of how life developed on Earth. Scientists are also learning about how **extraterrestrial** life might flourish in distant worlds.

Morning Glory Pool in Yellowstone National Park is home to extremophiles.

WHEN Do Stars Form?

Stars form when a thick cloud of dust and gas begins to collapse in on itself. When the dust and gas collide, gravity begins to mold all that material into a hot blob called a "protostar," which becomes a star.

The Beginning

The transformation from dust and gas to a protostar can take thousands of years. As that transformation takes place, the center of the newly forming star becomes so hot that it starts giving off light. Gravity continually forces the cloud of dust and gas to fall toward the protostar's super-hot center. For a star that grows to around the size of our sun, that process can take about a million years.

A star is born in an interstellar cloud.

FUN FACTS

- A star named Betelgeuse in the constellation Orion is known for both its size and brightness. Its diameter changes, but it is between 550 and 920 times the diameter of our sun and emits nearly 7,500 times as much energy.

- There are about 200 billion stars in the Milky Way galaxy.

The Middle

Gravity forces the new star to become hotter and smaller. The center of the star becomes so hot that fusion changes the hydrogen gas molecules into helium. That process takes about 20 million years and allows the star to shine for billions of years.

The End

Stars can be born. They can also die. As the core of a star collapses, it releases tons of energy and grows bigger and bigger. A very large star may explode into a supernova that will shine a billion times brighter than our sun before it finally fades from view. Only a few stars, however, ever become supernovae.

Supernova remnant

People Who Rocked the World

Edwin Hubble

Astronomer Edwin Hubble (1889–1953) used the strongest telescope available to discover that other galaxies existed beyond the Milky Way. He also proved that the universe is expanding and that distant stars and galaxies are continually moving farther away from us all the time. The Hubble Space Telescope, named for this visionary, now allows scientists to observe and photograph the most distant stars and galaxies. The telescope has circled Earth 110,000 times and snapped more than 570,000 pictures.

WHEN Do We See Shooting Stars?

Have you ever wished upon a falling, or shooting, star? It was actually a meteor, a small piece of rock or dust from space that is flying toward a planet or moon. When meteors hit Earth's atmosphere, they heat up because of **friction**. They usually burn up before they reach Earth's surface. When a meteor hits our atmosphere, its temperature may climb as high as 3,000°F (1,649°C).

Meteoroids and Meteorites

Meteoroids are bits and chunks of rock. Some are as small as a speck of sand; others are as large as a school bus. They can hurtle through space at speeds of 160,000 mph (257,495 kph)! When a meteoroid collides with Earth's atmosphere, it becomes a meteor. When a meteor crashes onto Earth, scientists call it a meteorite.

Comet flying across space

When It Rains, It Shines

Several times a year, meteor showers rain down on our planet in a blaze of streaking lights. Hundreds, sometimes thousands, of meteors can flame across the sky every hour. Meteors spend most of their time in deep space, but some come close enough to Earth that we can see them. They are often named after the constellation in which they seem to originate. Every November, the Leonid meteor shower appears in the constellation Leo.

Meteor showers happen every year when Earth crosses the dusty trail of an orbiting comet.

DID YOU KNOW?

Sometimes meteors are very noisy. On February 15, 2013, a massive meteor exploded over Russia, shattering windows and injuring more than 1,000 people.

WHEN Did the First Spacecraft Leave the Solar System?

On **August 20, 1977**, a spacecraft named *Voyager 2* was launched from Cape Canaveral, Florida. In **August 2012**, it left our solar system and set sail into **interstellar** space. It marked the first time in history that a spaceship left the sun's gravitational influence. This remarkable event took **35 years** to achieve.

Going, Going, Gone!

Voyager 2's sister ship, *Voyager 1*, followed right behind *Voyager 2*. Both ships are now headed out of the solar system and will continue to send back valuable information about outer space. When the two rockets blasted off for Jupiter and Saturn in the summer of 1977, the trip was supposed to last five years. Scientists now predict that the spaceships will run out of fuel in 2022. By that time, *Voyager 1* will be 12.4 billion miles (20 billion km) from the sun. *Voyager 2* will be about 10 billion miles (16 billion km) from the sun.

Milestones of *Voyager 1* and *2*

August 20
1977

NASA launches *Voyager 2* from Cape Canaveral Air Force Station in Florida. ▶

Voyager 2 blasts off.

September 5
1977

NASA launches *Voyager 1* from Cape Canaveral Air Force Station in Florida.

March 5
1979

Voyager 1 makes its closest approach to Jupiter. ▶

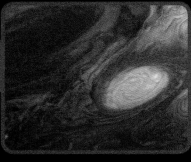
Jupiter, March 5, 1979

July 9
1979

Voyager 2 makes its closest approach to Jupiter.

November 12
1980

Voyager 1 flies by Saturn and begins its trip toward the edge of the solar system. ▶

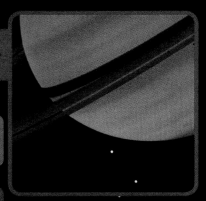

January 24
1986

Voyager 2 becomes the first spacecraft to travel near Uranus.

1987

Voyager 2 sees a star turning into a supernova.

Saturn with its two moons

1988

Voyager 2 sends the first color photos of Neptune back to Earth. ▶

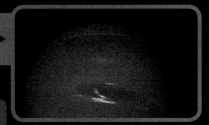
Voyager 2, Neptune

August 25
2012

Voyager 1 leaves the solar system and begins its voyage into interstellar space.

WHEN
Telescope Invented?

Telescopes are simple devices that make faraway objects look closer. It is a bit of a mystery just when the first telescope was invented. However, the first person to apply for a patent was Hans Lippershey, a Dutch eyeglass maker, in 1608.

Galileo

Others have taken credit for the telescope, but it was Galileo Galilei who put the instrument to good use. Galileo heard about the telescopes made by the Dutch and designed one of his own. When his was assembled, he pointed it toward the moon. He was astounded when he saw mountains and craters. He also discovered that the sun had spots on its surface and that Jupiter had moons of its own.

Galileo's telescope

Galileo demonstrating his telescope

Proved Right

Galileo lived at a time when the Catholic Church believed Earth was the center of the universe. The Church taught that the sun, moon, stars, and planets revolved around Earth. In 1543, Nicolaus Copernicus theorized that the planets, including Earth, revolved around the sun. No one really believed him, but Galileo and his telescope later proved Copernicus right. Around 1609, Johannes Kepler theorized that planets orbit the sun in paths that are not perfect circles.

Eyes on the Universe

Today, telescopes orbit high above Earth, giving astronomers amazing views of the universe. The Kepler space telescope has found many planets that orbit stars in our galaxy. Using information from Kepler, NASA scientists say about 8.8 billion stars in the Milky Way have planets where life might exist. These planets revolve around their suns in a so-called Goldilocks Zone. That means there's just the right amount of water, sunlight, and oxygen for life as we know it to thrive. Whether there is life on these planets is yet to be determined.

Kepler telescope

WHEN Was the Computer Invented?

In **1941**, a German engineer named Konrad Zuse built the first working programmable computer. It was called the Z3. Zuse had previously built two other **prototypes**, the Z1 and Z2. The Z3 did not look anything like modern computers. It was huge—larger than a couple of kitchen tables, and it weighed about a ton. The Z3 operated through a system of mechanical relays and switches. Engineers used this massive computer to help calculate and solve problems related to airplane design.

Konrad Zuse

30-Ton Super Brain

In **1943**, a company in the United States began building the world's first electronic computer. By **November 1945**, it unveiled the ENIAC, short for Electronic Numerical Integrator and Computer. Instead of using relays as switches, ENIAC used 18,000 **vacuum tubes**, similar to the tubes used in the first TV sets. ENIAC weighed 30 tons, but it proved that computers could be indispensable tools.

First computer circuit boards

Off to War

Early computers played an important role in World War II (1939–1945). The British used a computer called Colossus to break secret military codes sent by Nazi Germany, which Britain, the U.S., and other nations were fighting. The British used 10 Colossus computers, each containing 1,500 vacuum tubes. Although it took hours for the computers to break the Nazi codes, it would have taken humans weeks to accomplish the same task.

YOU DON'T SAY!

Microprocessors, which are no bigger than a human thumbnail, can run an entire computer. The tiny wonders also store and manage the data in the device.

We've Come a Long Way

Computer technology has changed dramatically over the past decade, and today's tiny processors can be put in anything, anywhere. Futurists predict that with advancing technology, space travel may become commonplace, machines will read our minds, and vehicles will drive themselves.

WHEN **Was the** First E-Mail Sent?

In 1971, Ray Tomlinson, a computer engineer working on what would become the Internet, sent the first e-mail—short for "electronic mail." While working on the Internet project, Tomlinson realized that there had to be a better way to leave messages on the computers of other scientists.

Tomlinson solved the problem by using the @ sign to target other computers on the system. The @ sign allowed Tomlinson to separate a computer user's address from the name of the network they were on. He began by sending messages between two computers that weren't that far apart. No one—not even Tomlinson—remembers what that historic message said.

Ray Tomlinson

An Electronic Revolution

It takes time to write a letter, mail it, and wait for a reply. E-mail allows people to communicate instantly. More than 1 billion people send e-mails every day. Today's e-mails include different kinds of attachments, including documents, videos, and pictures.

You've Got Mail

This is how e-mail gets from one computer to another.

1
You write a message to your friend. You then hit "Send."

2
Your message uploads to an e-mail server. Just like the U.S. Postal Service, the server locates your friend's address and sends the message.

3
Your message flies through the Internet.

4
Your message arrives at your friend's e-mail server, which delivers the mail to your friend's digital mailbox.

5
Your friend reads the e-mail.

Was the First Text Message Sent?

"Merry Christmas." So read the very first text message. A British engineer, Neil Papworth, sent it on December 3, 1992. When 22-year-old Papworth texted the holiday greeting from his computer to his boss's cell phone, he had no idea he had changed communication forever.

At the time, not many people carried cell phones, and no one texted. Today, some 63% of American teens text every day. Some teens send as many as 100 messages a day.

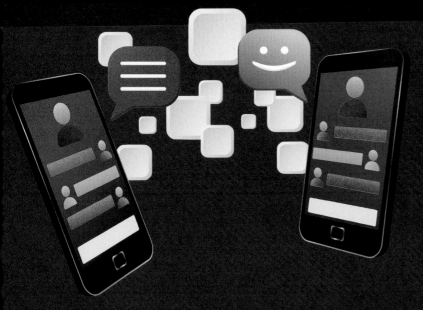

A New Language

Texting ushered in a new shorthand in which abbreviations substitute for words. Here's a smattering . . . LOL.

LOL—Laugh out loud
ROTFL—Rolling on the floor laughing
BFF—Best friends forever
AML—All my love
Thx—Thanks
RU—Are you
Gr8—Great
TTYL—Talk to you later
BBL—Be back later
XOXO—Hugs and kisses

When Was the First Tweet?

On March 21, 2006, Jack Dorsey, the founder of Twitter, tweeted the first tweet. "Just setting up my twttr," it said. Dorsey wanted Twitter to help groups of friends keep in touch. Tweeting quickly mushroomed into a new form of digital communication. It is similar to texting, but a tweet cannot contain more than 140 characters. Because of this, new tweeting **jargon** emerged.

Twitter soars high at the New York Stock Exchange

FUN FACTS

• Every second, 10 tweets mention Starbucks.

• When President Barack Obama won reelection in 2012, his victory tweet was re-tweeted more than 800,000 times—the record until 2014 when it was broken by Ellen DeGeneres' Oscar tweet. It generated more than 3.4 million re-tweets in one night!

• Nearly 21% of all Internet users around the world use Twitter.

• There were 13.7 million football tweets during the 2012 Super Bowl.

WHEN Was HDTV Invented?

Until the **mid-1960s**, most people could only watch TV in black and white. Then, color TV became all the rage. Today, high-definition television, HDTV, is starting to replace regular TV. Watching a high-definition television is a lot like going to the movies. Pictures are crisp and clear, and the sound can be ear splitting.

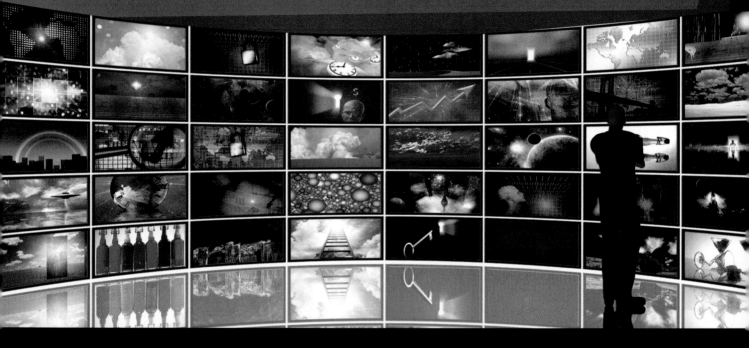

Long Time Coming

HDTVs work by picking up and decoding digital signals. When a TV station sends a high-definition signal, it is actually changing pictures and sounds into trillions of pieces of electronic data, called bits. HDTVs take that digital data and change it back into pictures and sounds. By 1981, people in the U.S. were able to watch HDTV, but only in demonstrations, not in their homes.

HDTV studio in Rockefeller Center, New York City

Bigger and Better

How are HDTVs different than regular TVs? Digital signals carry tons of information. HDTVs have more lines of information and pixels (tiny colored dots) per picture than standard TVs, making HDTV pictures sharper. Screens that take advantage of HDTV technology are usually wider and bigger, too. Some digital television sets send, store, and manipulate images, just like a computer. Curved screens and 4K ultra-high definition TVs have been introduced, and most HDTVs now have downloadable "apps" and Internet browsers.

The Next Big Thing

Just like the movies, TV has gone 3D. 3D technology relies on special glasses, and the experience involves both of your eyes receiving separate images. When the images reach your brain, they combine and create the **illusion** of a third **dimension**.

WHEN Did Smartphones Go on Sale?

The first text was sent in 1992. Today, people around the world are texting, sending photographs, taking videos, and browsing the Internet on handheld devices. While Apple Inc. made the smartphone common, its iPhone was not the first of its kind.

PDAs Meet Cell Phones

In the early 2000s, some people used cell phones, while others relied on personal digital assistants, or PDAs. Cell phones made telephone calls but did not do much else. PDAs, like the Palm Pilot, were personal organizers. You could take notes on a PDA, store contact information, write a to-do list, and **synchronize** the device with your computer.

In 1992, "The Simon" combined cell phones and PDAs. It was a mobile phone, a fax machine, and a personal assistant. At the time, Simon cost a whopping $899, which is probably one of the reasons few people bought it.

1991

1994

2000

2002

2004

2014

The BlackBerry

In 2002, a Canadian company came out with the BlackBerry 5810. Suddenly, millions of people around the world began using the phone to text, read e-mail, and surf the Web. If you wanted to phone someone, however, you had to plug the device into a headset.

Apple Steps In

Five years later, Apple came out with the iPhone. iPhone users could access the Internet at high speeds, make phone calls, take pictures, create videos, send text messages and e-mails . . . the list keeps growing.

People Who Rocked the World

Steve Jobs

As a child, Steve Jobs was not that interested in school. He liked to tinker with electronics. In high school, he and a buddy, Steve Wozniak, built a device that allowed them to make free long-distance telephone calls. They used their so-called Blue Box to phone the Vatican in Rome, Italy, where the pope lives. Jobs then went on to cofound Apple Inc., the technology company that gave the world Mac computers, iPads, iPhones, and other devices. These devices revolutionized the way we use information and how we communicate. When Jobs died in 2011, he was likely worth nearly $7 billion.

WHEN Was the First Video Game Introduced?

Ralph Baer

One day in 1966, Ralph Baer was sitting in his New Hampshire home watching TV. He asked himself: What else could a person do with a television besides watch it? Why not play games? Baer, who worked as an engineer for the military, jotted down some notes. Soon after, the video game industry was born.

The First Console

Baer helped design the first video game console. It was made from vacuum tubes and plugged into a television. Players could chase one another using two squares. By the 1970s, Baer had refined his "Brown Box," which became the Magnavox Odyssey, the first video game console sold in stores. Players could plug in six game **cartridges** to play up to 12 games. The system, however, was not very popular.

Odyssee
Das elektronische Fernsehspiel für die ganze Familie

The Magnavox Odyssey was sold around the world, with games in several languages including German.

Pong

Games changed quickly. Along came Atari, a cartridge-based video game system in which players could play multiple games. Atari's *Pong*, introduced in 1972, was the first successful commercial video game. The Atari console became a best seller. The company produced other games, including *Space Invaders*, *Missile Command*, and *Combat*.

On the Go!

Many families have or have heard of the Nintendo 2DS or the PlayStation Vita. The Nintendo Game Boy, the first handheld game console, came before. With its black-and-white screen, Game Boy was a huge success when it first went on sale in 1989. Its most popular game was *Tetris*. Game Boy, however, was not the first programmable handheld game console. That honor belongs to Milton Bradley's Microvision, which came out in 1979.

Best-Selling Video Games

1 **Wii Sports**
Nintendo—82 million copies
2 **Super Mario Bros.**
Nintendo—40 million copies
3 **Tetris**
Game Boy—35 million copies
4 **Super Mario World**
Nintendo—21 million copies
5 **Kinect Adventures**
Xbox—18 million copies

Source: London Daily Telegram

Boy playing video golf using a Nintendo Wii

WHEN Were Digital Cameras Invented?

Digital cameras are everywhere, including inside cell phones. The technology began to be developed some 50 years ago when NASA started using digital signals to relay information from its space probes back to Earth.

No More Film

In 1972, Texas Instruments patented the first camera that didn't need film. In 1981, Sony developed a camera that recorded pictures onto a minidisc. The photographer could then put the disc into a reader that was connected to a TV monitor or color printer. The first digital camera that worked with a home computer went on sale in 1994.

How Do They Work?

In the past, cameras took photos on film, which had to be chemically processed in order for the image to appear. Digital cameras have a minicomputer inside them. The computer records the image electronically. Like a film camera, a digital camera has a series of **lenses** that focus light to create an image. Instead of projecting that light onto film, the camera electronically breaks the light down into digital data.

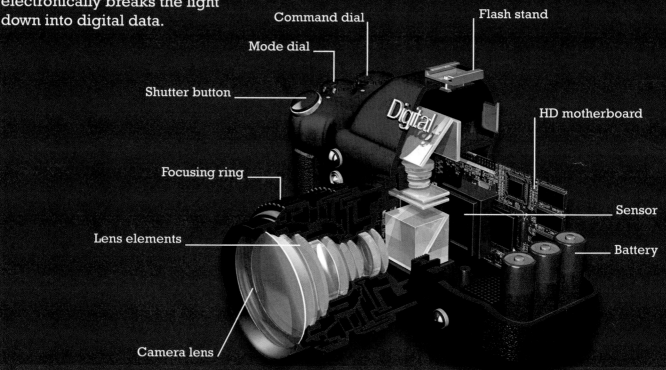

- Command dial
- Mode dial
- Flash stand
- Shutter button
- HD motherboard
- Focusing ring
- Sensor
- Lens elements
- Battery
- Camera lens

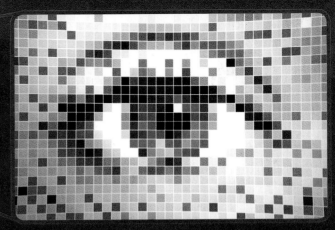

Human eye in pixels

TRY IT!

The images from a digital camera are made up of pixels, which are very small dots. The more pixels an image has, the sharper the picture. See for yourself.

What You Will Need
• Graph paper
• Fine-point black pen

Step 1

Fill in the squares of the graph paper to represent a letter. In this case, we used the letter L. Each square represents one pixel. Fill in blocks in an area five blocks high and three blocks wide.

Step 2

Repeat Step 1. This time, fill in the blocks in an area seven blocks high and five blocks wide.

Step 3

Repeat the step again, using an area nine blocks high and seven blocks wide.

Step 4

Compare the images. Which is the clearest?

WHEN Did the First Talking Robot Go into Space?

In August 2013, a 13-inch-high Japanese robot named Kirobo became the first talking robot to circle the planet. Kirobo's destination was the International Space Station.

The robot's mission was to see how humans and robots got along with one another on long space voyages. Once Kirobo arrived at the space station, it said, "Good morning to everyone on Earth," in Japanese. Another pint-sized digital robot named Mirata was listening to the transmission back on Earth.

On August 4, 2013, the Japanese Aerospace Exploration Agency launched a rocket carrying **cargo** for the International Space Station. Besides the robot, the rocket carried daily supplies for the astronauts, spare parts, and other necessary research equipment. The robot was intended to be a companion to the Japanese astronaut on board the Space Shuttle.

I, Robot

Most robots are controlled by computers. Some are designed to perform difficult physical tasks, while others are designed to solve complicated **calculations**. The first industrial robot was built in **1954** by a self-taught inventor named George C. Devol. The digitally operated and programmable robot was a mechanical arm like those now widely used in car manufacturing and other industries.

Devol named his creation the Universal Automation, which was later shortened to Unimation and then again to Unimate. Unimate's first job was at a General Motors plant in New Jersey, where it was programmed to lift metal parts taken from hot die-cast molds. Unimate laid the foundation for the robotics industry.

Robots in the workplace

A Look Back

The first robot rolled off an assembly line in Japan in **1932**. "Lilliput" was a wind-up toy that could walk. It stood just six inches tall.

A Look Forward

Science students in Switzerland are working on a turtle-shaped bot that can swim underwater while carrying cargo. The Turtlebot uses flippers, just like a live turtle, to propel itself through the water.

WHEN Was Popcorn Discovered?

The next time you dig into a bucket of popcorn, consider this: People in Peru were eating the tasty treat some 6,000 years ago. Scientists at the Smithsonian Institution in Washington, D.C., found evidence of the oldest known corncobs and husks at two locations along Peru's northern coast.

America's Food

Corn, or maize, has been a dietary **staple** of Native Americans for centuries. The corn you eat at picnics and festivals was first cultivated in Mexico about 9,000 years ago. It came from its wild cousin, a plant called *balsas teosinte*. By the time Christopher Columbus made his way to the Americas in 1492, maize was a critical crop. Native Americans greeted Columbus wearing necklaces made of popcorn.

Primitive Popcorn

Early Native Americans lit a fire over sand, and when the sand was hot enough, they threw corn kernels on top and popped them.

A Popcorn Banquet

At the first Thanksgiving in 1621, according to the legend, the Pilgrims nibbled on popcorn after a Native American named Quadequina poured a **bushel** of it onto the dinner table. The popcorn was a big hit. According to one dinner guest, the food was "unseen and unknown by most of the Pilgrims." Unlike our current holiday, that first Thanksgiving feast lasted for three days.

FUN FACTS

- The heaviest popcorn ball on record weighed just over 3,400 pounds.

- The average American eats 51 quarts of popcorn a year.

- In 2012, nearly a billion pounds of packaged popcorn was sold.

WHEN Was Ice Cream First Served?

Some date the discovery of ice cream back to the 4th century B.C. Others trace it back to the 2nd century B.C., when Alexander the Great, king of Macedonia and conqueror of the Persian Empire, ate snow flavored with honey.

One **legend** states that Nero, an ancient Roman emperor, sent slaves into the mountains for snow, which he then mixed with fruit and honey. Others claim China's rulers ate ice cream nearly 1,400 years ago.

Alexander the Great
(356 B.C.–323 B.C.)

Dessert Is Served

The New World's first written account of ice cream appeared in 1744, when the colonial governor of Maryland, Thomas Bladen, served the treat with strawberries and milk. Nearly 100 years later, a dairyman by the name of Jacob Fussell opened the first ice cream factory.

Throughout history, many famous people have enjoyed a dish or two of the sweet treat.

- **Marco Polo:** The great traveler brought a sherbet recipe from the Far East back to Italy.

- **George Washington:** The father of our country had two pewter ice cream pots at his Mount Vernon estate.

- **Thomas Jefferson:** The third United States president had an 18-step recipe for ice cream that closely resembled a dessert called Baked Alaska.

- **Dolley Madison:** On **March 4, 1813**, the wife of President James Madison was the first to serve ice cream in the White House.

Dolley Madison

DID YOU KNOW?

Grocery stores didn't start selling ice cream until the 1930s.

Ice cream on display in Paris

WHEN Did People Start Eating Peanut Butter?

Most people credit George Washington Carver with the invention of peanut butter. While the great scientist did have a hand in making peanut butter popular, the Aztecs first invented the spread.

Peanuts in America

By the **1300s**, the Aztec Empire stretched from central Mexico south to present-day Guatemala. The Aztecs ground roasted peanuts into a paste, but they were probably not the first to use the peanut. As early as **1500 B.C.**, Incas living in Peru used these nuts as sacrificial offerings, and Native Americans in Brazil ground peanuts and mixed them with maize to make a hearty drink.

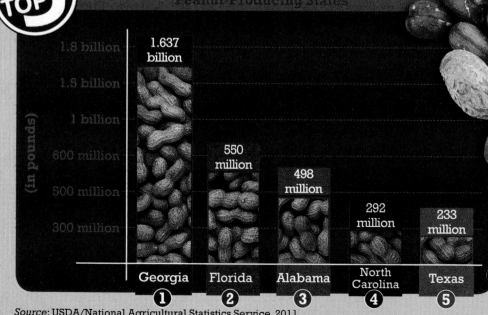

TOP 5 — Peanut-Producing States

(in pounds)

State	Amount	Rank
Georgia	1.637 billion	1
Florida	550 million	2
Alabama	498 million	3
North Carolina	292 million	4
Texas	233 million	5

Source: USDA/National Agricultural Statistics Service, 2011

So Smooth

In 1884, a Canadian named Marcellus Gilmore Edson created a peanut paste by roasting milled peanuts between two heated surfaces. Twelve years later, Dr. John Kellogg, who became famous for his cereal products, developed a way to make peanut butter from raw peanuts. Smooth peanut butter was the **brainchild** of Joseph Rosefield, who found a way to keep peanut oil from separating. He licensed his invention to a company called Peter Pan. Rosefield then formed his own peanut butter company, which sold Skippy Peanut Butter.

People Who Rocked the World

George Washington Carver

George Washington Carver (1861–1943), who had been born a slave, developed more than 300 products from peanuts. After graduating from college, Carver studied various plants and different ways to use land for farming. In 1916, he published *How to Grow the Peanut and 105 Ways of Preparing it for Human Consumption*. His publication helped launch the peanut industry in the South, saving the economy in that area.

WHEN Was Pizza Invented?

Pizza was commonly served in Naples, Italy, by the 1700s, providing an inexpensive meal to many hungry mouths. Now there's thick Sicilian pie, New York-style slices, and deep-dish Chicago pizza to please your palate.

Pizza Delivery

Pizza was originally a simple flatbread topped with a variety of things, including tomatoes, cheese, anchovies, and garlic. Sold by street **vendors**, pizza was eaten for any meal, including breakfast.

Margherita Pizza

In 1889, Queen Margherita visited Naples and sampled a variety of pizzas. She especially liked one topped with soft white mozzarella cheese, tomatoes, and green basil. That style of pizza became known as the Margherita. It is said the queen liked the dish not only for its taste, but because the color of the toppings reflected the Italian flag—red, white, and green.

Queen Margherita

New World Pizza

When Italian **immigrants** came to the U.S. in the early 1900s, they brought one of their favorite foods. The **enticing** smell of baking pizzas in many Italian neighborhoods soon spread, and the pizza craze caught on. The first pizzeria in the U.S. is said to be a New York City restaurant named Lombardi's. It received its license to sell pizza in 1905. Lombardi's still makes pizzas, although not at its original Spring Street location.

YOU DON'T SAY!

Here are a few popular pizza toppings from around the globe.

- **India:** pickled ginger and *paneer* (a form of cottage cheese)
- **Russia:** *mockba*—a combination of sardines, tuna, mackerel, salmon, and onion
- **Brazil:** green peas
- **Japan:** eel, squid, and a combination of mayonnaise, potato, and bacon
- **France:** a mixture of bacon, onion, and fresh cream
- **Pakistan:** curry
- **Australia:** shrimp, pineapple, and barbecue sauce
- **Costa Rica:** coconut
- **Netherlands:** double meat, double cheese, and double onion
- **United States:** pepperoni, mushroom, sausage, green pepper, and extra cheese

Source: TLC.com

WHEN Was the First Sandwich Made?

You can thank a member of the British nobility for inventing the sandwich. John Montagu was the fourth Earl of Sandwich and served as the British first lord of the Admiralty during the American Revolution (1775–1783).

One of his favorite meals was slices of meat between two pieces of bread. According to legend, the earl liked the meal because he could play cards and eat without getting his hands sticky with meat grease. Other people thought this was a good idea, too. They began to order "the same as Sandwich."

John Montagu

Meal of the Worker

The sandwich became popular during the **Industrial Revolution** in Europe and the U.S., when the use of factories and machines began to build up the workforce. Factory workers found that sandwiches were easily **transportable**—they could quickly pack their meals at home and bring them to work.

From Shellfish to Cheese

American cookbooks began highlighting sandwich recipes in   . People weren't just putting meat between slices of bread; some recipes called for fruit, cheese, nuts, mushrooms, and shellfish. After the U.S. Civil War   , sandwiches were served in both high-class restaurants and run-down taverns.

FU FACTS

Across the U.S., sandwiches go by many names.

- **Hoagie:** The hoagie supposedly originated in Philadelphia as a staple lunch for Italian workers at the Hog Island shipyards.

- **Sub:** One myth claims the name originated in New London, Connecticut, when nearby shipyard workers ordered sandwiches from a shopkeeper who called them "subs" because they were shaped like submarines.

- **Hero:** Supposedly the name "hero" first appeared in the *New York Tribune* in 1936. The writer said the sandwich was so large "you had to be a hero to eat it."

- **Po' Boy or Poor Boy:** During a trolley car strike in New Orleans, Louisiana, in 1929, two brothers, Clovis and Bennie Martin, sent sandwiches to striking workers in the city, poor boys, who were not only out of work but also out of money.

WHEN Did People Start Eating Candy?

In 2011, candy sales in the U.S. topped $32 billion. That's 25 pounds of candy for every man, woman, and child in the country. Candy was once only enjoyed by the rich. In the 19th century, however, the price of sugar dropped, and candy became affordable for everyone.

How Sweet It Is

While many civilizations made sweet treats from fruits, nuts, and honey, the history of modern candy is deeply rooted in the history of sugar. Sugarcane was harvested on the Pacific Island of New Guinea 10,000 years ago. Island residents picked the plant and ate it raw, chewing the stem until a burst of sugary flavor filled their mouths.

Sugar, Sugar

Sugar was refined as it moved from continent to continent. By the year 600, Persian rulers entertained guests with a variety of sugary sweets. Arab traders brought sugar with them throughout Asia and northern Africa. The word *candy* comes from the Arabic word "qandi," which means "made from sugar."

Europe Gets a Taste

When Europeans traveled to the Jerusalem during the **Crusades**, they brought back stories of sugar. Christopher Columbus brought the plant to the New World, and soon the West Indies was covered in sweet sugarcane fields.

Bar None

In its pure form, chocolate is bitter. In 1875, a friend of Henry Nestle named Daniel Peter had a sweet idea. He added Nestle condensed milk to chocolate, which cut down the bitter taste. The chocolate industry was forever changed. In 1893, Milton Hershey saw a chocolate-making machine at the Chicago World's Fair. Since he was already making caramel candy, he thought he might as well make chocolate candy, too. Within a year, Hershey had invented the world's first chocolate bar—the Hershey Bar.

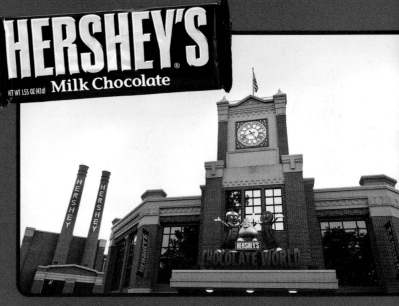

Chocolate World, in Hershey, Pennsylvania

TOP 5

Best-Selling Candies of All Time

1 M&M's: The tiny drop that "melts in your mouth, not in your hand" dates back to 1941.

2 Hershey's Kiss: First introduced in 1907, no one knows how it got its name.

3 Snickers: Released in 1930, the name came from Ethel Mars's favorite horse. Ethel was married to Franklin Mars, owner of the Mars candy company.

4 Twizzlers: "Twizzlers brand" twisted licorice was developed in 1845, the same year that rubber bands were invented.

5 Reese's Peanut Butter Cups: Cooked up in 1928, Reese's makes so many peanut butter cups each year that every person in the U.S., Japan, Europe, Africa, China, Australia, and India could eat one.

WHEN Was the First Hamburger Served?

Who served up the first burger? Many people claim the honor.

LOUIS LUNCH   EST. 1895

Louis' Lunch

On Crown Street in New Haven, Connecticut, there's a small eatery called Louis' Lunch. As the story goes, in **1900**, someone walked into the restaurant and asked the owner, Louis Lassen, for something quick to eat. Louis saw some ground steak in the kitchen. He cooked it up and put it between two slices of toast. The hamburger was born, or at least one version of it. Louis' Lunch is still around. You can't buy a burger on a bun at Louis' Lunch, though—only on toast.

Uncle Fletcher

Fletcher Davis, also known as "Uncle Fletcher," is said to have invented the hamburger in the 1880s. According to legend, Uncle Fletcher brought his sandwich to the St. Louis World's Fair in 1904, where the sandwich was given the name "hamburger."

Charlie Nagreen sold meatballs. He put them on two pieces of bread in 1885 for the people of Seymour, Wisconsin. That same year, brothers Frank and Charles Menches sold a ground beef sandwich in Hamburg, New York, near Buffalo. Hamburg claims fame as the home of the hamburger.

The McDonald's Museum is a re-creation of the first eat-in McDonald's Restaurant, which opened on April 15, 1955, in Des Plaines, Illinois.

WHEN Was the First Hot Dog Served?

Sausages have been around since **antiquity**, but Germany takes credit for inventing the most popular sausage of all—the hot dog. They called it the "dachshund," or "little-dog" sausage.

You Say Wiener, I Say Frankfurter

The origins of the hot dog have been disputed for centuries. The people of Frankfurt, Germany, say the hot dog, or "frankfurter," was invented in their city in 1487. Others claim the wiener was first cooked up in Vienna, Austria.

Hot dog stand, New York City

On a Bun

European immigrants brought the hot dog to the U.S. Some say the first person to put it on a bun was a German push-cart vendor who sold the sausages with rolls and sauerkraut in New York City.

Charles Feltman opened the first hot dog stand on Coney Island in 1871. Allegedly, he sold more than 3,600 hot dogs his first year.

"Get Your Red Hots!"

When did the frankfurter, dachshund, little-dog, wiener, sausage become a hot dog? Some say the name came when vendors at the New York Polo Grounds hawked sausages on a cold April day as the city's beloved Giants were playing baseball.

Supposedly, the vendors shouted, "They're red hot! Get your dachshund sausages while they're red hot." A cartoonist from the *New York Journal* witnessed the exchange and drew a cartoon for the newspaper. He didn't know how to spell *dachshund*, so he simply wrote "hot dog" in his drawing. Historians doubt the **accuracy** of this story because they have yet to find the cartoon.

The "Wienermobile" promotes and advertises Oscar Mayer products.

WHEN Was the Steamboat Invented?

Residents of New York City were treated to a very unusual sight on the afternoon of AUGUST 17, 1807. On the East River, a strange looking boat began to belch flame and smoke from a tall smokestack. On the side of the ship's hull were two paddle wheels. At about 1 p.m., the ship left its **moorings** and steamed into history books as the first successful voyage of a commercial steamboat.

Though it was Robert Fulton who ran that first successful steamboat service, the steamboat was actually invented by John Fitch in 1787.

Robert Fulton

Up the Hudson

On that day, the steamship journeyed up the Hudson River at a rate of 5 mph (8 kph). Twenty-four hours later, it arrived at the manor house of Robert Livingston, some 110 miles (177 km) upstream. The ship departed the next day for Albany and then returned to New York City. The entire voyage took five days.

Fast and Reliable

Before the development of the steamboat, ships were powered by wind. Flatboats and keelboats pulled by pack animals or powered by human muscle moved goods and people slowly down canals. The steamboat made traveling easier and allowed goods, such as cotton, food, flour, and lumber, to be transported to far-off destinations with ease and speed.

It spurred the American economy. New towns sprang up along the great rivers, fueled by the new trade.

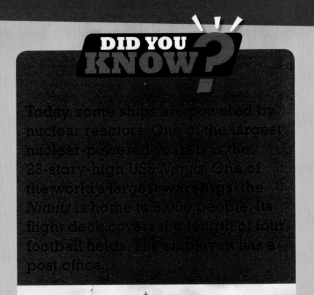

DID YOU KNOW?

Today, some ships are powered by nuclear reactors. One of the largest nuclear-powered vessels is the 23-story-high USS *Nimitz*. One of the world's largest warships, the *Nimitz* is home to 6,000 people. Its flight deck covers the length of four football fields. The ship even has a post office.

Did the *Titanic* Sink?

Perhaps no shipwreck has captured people's imagination as much as the *Titanic*. Weighing in at 46,329 tons, the ship was supposed to be unsinkable. The *Titanic* left Southampton, England, on April 10, 1912, bound for New York City. At 11:40 p.m. on April 14, 1912, some 380 miles southeast of Newfoundland, Canada, the ocean liner struck an **iceberg**. The impact damaged the ship, and in less than three hours, it broke in half and plunged more than two miles to the ocean floor.

Watery Graves

The shipwreck resulted in the deaths of 1,522 people. Only 705 passengers and crew members survived. Scientists now believe that the large hole was not the cause of the disaster, but rather six small slits sank the *Titanic*. Tiny metal fasteners, called rivets, held the ship together. When the *Titanic* hit the iceberg, the brittle heads of the rivets broke off, causing the great ship to sink.

Other Notable Sea Disasters

May 29 1914

Empress of Ireland: 1,012 dead

May 7 1915

Lusitania: About 1,200 people lost their lives when the ship sank.

July 24 1915

SS Eastland: 844 dead

January 30 1945

Wilhelm Gustloff: 5,000–9,000 dead

July 25 1956

Andrea Doria and *Stockholm:* More than 50 dead.

December 20 1987

Doña Paz: 4,047 dead

On May 7, 1915, a German World War I submarine torpedoed the British passenger ship SS *Lusitania* off the coast of Ireland. The ship sank just 18 minutes after it was attacked. About 1,200 people were killed, including 128 Americans. This tragedy outraged Americans and encouraged the United States to join World War I.

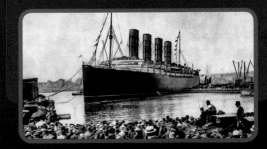

On July 25, 1956, the 697-foot-long (212 meters) *Andrea Doria* was carrying 1,700 passengers and crew. It collided with a smaller ship, the *Stockholm*, which had 500 passengers and crew. Dozens of people died that day, but heroic rescue efforts saved the lives of most people on board both ships.

WHEN Was the First Motorcycle Built?

Many people credit Gottlieb Daimler with inventing the first motorcycle in 1885. Daimler took a gasoline-powered engine and put it on a wooden-frame bicycle, known as the "bone crusher," because of its jarring ride. He placed two small wheels on the outside of the bike, and it became a motorcycle. Later, he went on to make automobiles.

Internal Combustion

At the heart of Daimler's bone crusher, and most other vehicles of the time, was the internal **combustion** engine, in which gasoline mixes with air. Inside the engine, a spark from a spark plug ignites the mixture, which causes the gasoline to explode. During the 1860s and 1870s, many people found innovative ways to turn these explosions into mechanical energy that could power machines and vehicles.

Two-Wheeled Drive

In 1892, the Millet became the first successful two-wheeled motorbike. Previous two-wheeled designs had failed because the bikes tipped over. This bike, however, stayed upright despite the five-cylinder rotary engine in the hub of its rear wheel.

The Millet motorcycle

Though motorcycles look sleek, they are really complex machines. Here are a few of their many parts.

The fuel tank holds the gasoline that powers the machine.

The seat is designed to be as comfortable as possible for the driver.

The throttle controls the power of the engine.

The drive chain transfers power from the engine and gearbox to the rear wheel.

Foot pegs are located on either side of the bike.

The engine is the bike's powerhouse.

Exhaust pipes release waste gas into the atmosphere after the gasoline burns.

The front forks connect the bike frame to the front wheel.

A racer competes in the Brazil Cup of Freestyle Motocross in Rio de Janeiro, Brazil.

WHEN Did People Begin Riding on Trains?

Which was faster, a steam locomotive or a horse? On August 28, 1830, Peter Cooper's steam locomotive *Tom Thumb* and a horse named Lightning lined up side-by-side—*Tom Thumb* on its tracks pulling a wagonload of people, the horse on the ground strapped to a carriage. Lightning beat Cooper's "teakettle on a track." The train had led the race until it was stopped by mechanical failure.

Trains were soon moving Americans across the continent. By 1835, there were more than 1,000 miles (1,609 km) of railroad track in the U.S., mostly along the East Coast.

The Start of Steam Power

Before the train, people traveled by boat, carriage, and horse. Roads and trails were often muddy and impassable, which made travel slow and difficult. In the late 1700s, a Scottish inventor named James Watt built the first modern steam engine. In 1804, Englishman Richard Trevithick used that engine to invent the first steam locomotive. Trevithick's train was powerful enough to pull 10 tons and 70 people. Though early steam locomotives frequently broke down, they were less expensive to repair and maintain than feeding and caring for horses.

A Look Back

Steam trains were fueled by coal or wood, which revolutionized transportation. Steam traveled through pipes to cylinders, which had valves that helped the train go backward and forward. Steam moved the cylinders, which contained **pistons**, up and down. Connecting rods drove the train's wheels, while excess steam vented out a smokestack.

A Look Forward

The train of the future might be the hyperloop. The futuristic concept shown in an image, below, would have pods that can carry people through tubes at super-fast speeds up to 760 miles (1,223 km) per hour. The pods would levitate on a cushion of air, much like an air hockey puck.

High-speed commuter train

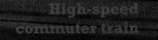

WHEN Did People Begin Riding in Cars?

In the late 1800s, the "horseless carriage" ran on steam. The first automobiles were large and odd-looking—some resembled sleighs on wheels. As cars evolved, so did the fuels that powered them. Historians credit Karl Friedrick Benz and Gottlieb Daimler with the idea of powering a motorcar with gasoline. They filed **patents** for a gasoline-powered automobile on January 29, 1886, in two different German cities. Benz's model, which he first drove in 1885, had three wheels. Daimler's car was the first four-wheeled auto.

Daimler takes a ride in his car.

Henry Ford

While many people had a hand in inventing the automobile, there was only one man who made it affordable. An engineer named Henry Ford built his first automobile in 1896. He called it the "Quadricycle" because it ran on four bicycle tires. Ford opened his motorcar company in 1903.

On the Line and All One Color

At first, Ford built only a few cars a day, and few American families could afford to own one. Then, Henry Ford devised the **assembly line** method of **mass production** for manufacturing cars, which cut their price substantially. Ford also cut costs by making all Model T cars the same. Ford once said that customers could get the Model T in any color they wanted—as long as it was black.

Ford's assembly line went into production in 1913. Ropes pulled the frame of a car past a line of workers, and each worker added a part to the car. This cut the amount of time it took to make a car from 12 hours to 93 minutes. Ford sold 15 million Model T's in 19 years. Today's assembly lines, although similar in idea to Ford's, are highly mechanized.

Replica of a 1923 Model T Ford

FUN FACTS

In August 1888, Karl Benz's wife, Bertha, drove her husband's prototype "motorwagen" from Mannheim, Germany, to her mother's house in Pforzheim, a distance of some 60 miles (97 km).

WHEN Did the First Drive-Through Open?

For decades, people packed lunches to eat as they motored down our nation's roads. Roadside restaurants and motels were not common, as they are today. Legend has it that Sheldon "Red" Chaney opened Red's Giant Hamburg in Springfield, Missouri, the first fast-food restaurant with a drive-through window, in 1947.

As the story goes, Chaney, who ran a gas station, decided to sell hamburgers to hungry motorists traveling down Route 66. The business thrived for years, but closed when Chaney retired in 1984.

Vince Hanneman shows off his masterpiece, the Cathedral of Junk.

Roadside Attractions

Roadside attractions sprang up when people began driving for pleasure. Without having to stray too far from the road, people stopped to see strange things, natural or otherwise, such as the Tiniest Church in Yuma, Arizona, or oversized, fake dinosaurs in Michigan. Vince Hanneman's Cathedral of Junk in Austin, Texas, was built one hubcap or toilet urinal at a time.

The First Motel

The first motel opened on December 12, 1925, in San Luis Obispo, California. Arthur Heineman named his business "Motor Hotel." Its Spanish-style bell tower and sign can still be seen today, though the sign is not the original.

FUN FACTS

The first drive-in theater opened in 1933 in Camden, New Jersey. Richard Hollingshead charged between 25 cents and $1 per car. By 1938, most cities had drive-in theaters. By 1963, 3,502 drive-in theaters were in operation across the country.

Curbside dining means not having to leave your car.

WHEN Were Other Major Milestones in Transportation?

First, people walked. Then, they harnessed the power of animals to travel from place to place. Today, people can move faster than the speed of sound. How did we get here? Here are some other major transportation **milestones**.

The Pony Express

On April 3, 1860, the Pony Express began delivering mail between St. Joseph, Missouri, and Sacramento, California, roughly 2,000 miles (3,219 km) apart. It previously took three weeks for a letter from Missouri to reach California. The Pony Express, using riders on about 400 horses, cut the time to 10 days. But the system was too expensive and was shut down in less than two years.

Transcontinental Railroad

On May 10, 1869, railroad officials hammered a golden spike into the train track at Promontory Summit in Utah. The Transcontinental Railroad was officially open for business. The railroad physically connected the east and west coasts of the U.S. People, goods, and resources could now be easily transported across the country. The telegraph that announced the end of the project to an anxious nation had a very short, one-word message: "Done!"

Railroad officials drive the golden stake.

Interstate Highways

President Dwight D. Eisenhower created the interstate highway system when he signed the Federal-Aid Highway Act of 1956. The law **authorized** the creation of 41,000 miles (66,000 km) of highways that, the President said, would make traveling easier and safer.

High-Speed Rail

The high-speed Maglev train, which travels at over 300 mph (483 kph), debuted in 2002 in Shanghai, China. Instead of running on electricity or diesel fuel, powerful magnets propel Maglev trains at high speeds. And instead of riding on rails, the trains ride on a cushion of air.

Chinese high-speed train

WHEN Was the Flying Car Invented?

In 1989, Paul Moller showed off the world's first flying car. The Skycar has undergone many revisions since its **inception**. The current model has eight engines, two flight computers, and powerful fans that generate enough thrust to lift the 2,400-pound vehicle into the air.

The Skycar was built to travel up to 375 mph (604 kph). In 2013, Moller partnered with a California technology company to get the car up in the air.

Amphibious Cars

In 2003, an **amphibious** car was test-driven across the Thames River in London, England. The Aquada Sports Amphibian can race down a highway at 100 mph (161 kph), or use jets to splash through water at 30 mph (48 kph). Previous amphibious cars could only motor across the water at about 6 mph (9.7 kph).

Cars of the Future

Could you or your grandchildren one day drive one of these sci-fi cars?

1 Driverless Car: Leave the driving to a robot. That's what Mercedes-Benz hopes drivers will be able to do in the future. The company is working on a robo car that doesn't need a human driver.

2 Water for Fuel: Scientists are working on creating cars that run on water.

3 Liquid Air: Cars that run on liquid air function somewhat like a steam engine. Instead of steam, the car uses cold air. Air turns into liquid nitrogen at super-freezing temperatures of $-320°F$ ($-160°C$). When the air warms up, it begins to boil, eventually turning into a gas that can pump the car's pistons.

4 Grease Lightning: Some automobiles are fueled by cooking oil. It's cheap and burns clean.

5 Air Pressure: Compressed air can power your car. A hydraulic pump forces compressed air against a fluid that turns the wheels.

FUN FACTS

There are approximately 1 billion cars in the world. The U.S. is the leader in the number of cars on the road, with 1.3 people for every car in the country. In China, there are approximately 6.5 people per car.

WHEN Did the Egyptians Build the Pyramids of Giza?

Beginning about **5,500 years ago**, cities grew up along Egypt's Nile River, and the ancient Egyptian civilization was born. It lasted **3,000 years**. Perhaps the best-known gifts of the Egyptians are the great pyramids of Giza. These huge pyramids, which served as **tombs**, are now more than **4,000 years old**.

The Pharaohs

Ancient Egypt was ruled by kings and queens called **pharaohs** from until , when Alexander the Great of Macedonia conquered Egypt, and the last Egyptian dynasty ended. When Alexander died in , Ptolemy, one of Alexander's generals, founded a new dynasty in Egypt. Cleopatra, the last ruler of the Macedonian dynasty and the last Egyptian queen, ruled from .

King Tutankhamun's funeral mask

Pyramids in the Giza desert

TRY IT!

The ancient Egyptians are famous for their mummies. You can make a mummy with an apple.

What You Will Need
- knife ⚠️
- apple
- plastic bowl
- measuring cup
- baking soda
- salt

Step 1

Carefully cut the apple into four pieces. Put one piece in a plastic bowl.

Step 2

Mix one cup of baking soda with one cup of salt. Pour the mixture over the apple within the plastic bowl.

Step 3

Store the plastic bowl in a dry, dark place. Eat the rest of the apple while it is fresh. One week later, check the apple in the plastic bowl.

⚠️ Never use a knife without adult supervision!

FUN FACTS

- When a pharaoh died, the Egyptians buried the king or queen with furniture, gold, jewelry, and food to bring to the afterlife.

- The Great Pyramid at Giza, the largest of Egypt's 70 pyramids, is 481 feet (147 m) tall. It is made out of 2.3 million stone blocks, each weighing about two tons.

WHEN Did Ancient Greek City-States Exist?

Unlike other ancient civilizations, the ancient Greeks did not create a vast empire. Instead, they built small, independent city-states. Each had its own government and culture. The rise of the city-states began around 750 B.C.

Greek Monuments

The Greeks were known for their **architecture**. They also worshipped many gods, including Athena, the goddess of wisdom, civilization, arts, and literature. The Parthenon, a temple that sits atop the Acropolis in Athens, Greece, was finished in 432 B.C. and was dedicated to Athena. The columns of the temple were constructed of white marble, and they glistened in the sun. Today, the Parthenon is a symbol of ancient Greek culture.

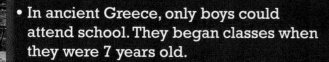

FUN FACTS

- In ancient Greece, only boys could attend school. They began classes when they were 7 years old.

- The Greeks invented theater and put on plays during religious festivals. The Greeks also built **amphitheaters,** where the plays were staged.

- When Greeks became ill, they thought they were being punished by the gods.

This statue of Melpomene, the muse of tragedy in Greek theater, was made in 50 B.C.

Greek Tales

The ancient Greeks are known for their **mythology**. Here are a few of their famous tales.

Pandora's Box

Pandora was the first woman on Earth. Zeus, the most powerful god, gave her a box and told her never to open it. But Pandora did open it, and when she did, she unleashed all the troubles humans face today.

Trojan Horse

The Greeks and the Trojans, neighbors from the city of Troy, had battled for years. Then, the Greeks suddenly surrendered and presented the Trojans with a huge wooden horse as a gift. The Trojans brought the horse inside their city walls. Once inside the city, the Greek Army climbed out of the hollow horse and defeated their enemy.

King Midas

King Midas wished that everything he touched would turn to gold. When his wish was granted, even his food and his daughter turned to gold. The god who granted the wish took pity on Midas and reversed the magic. Midas became a poor but very happy man.

155

WHEN Did the Ancient Romans Rule the World?

Rome was the world's largest and longest-lasting empire. The ancient Roman Empire existed from 27 B.C. to 476 A.D. By 50 B.C., the empire stretched across Europe, Northern Africa, and parts of the Middle East. By 200 A.D., wars with northern **"barbarians"** weakened the empire, which completely collapsed in 476 A.D.

Roman coin with the bust of Caesar Augustus (30 B.C.–14 A.D.)

Early Republic

Before Rome was a great empire, it was a small city on the Italian peninsula. In 509 B.C., the Romans established a republic where there were no kings or queens. The Roman Senate made laws and controlled the government.

Typical suit of armor of a Roman soldier

Major Moments in the History of Ancient Rome

753 B.C.
Rome is founded.

146 B.C.
Romans defeat Carthage in the Third Punic War, taking over territory in northern Africa.

32–31 B.C.
Roman warrior Octavian defeats the Egyptian queen Cleopatra in battle. A year later, Egypt becomes part of the Roman Empire.

Powerful Army

The Romans ruled a vast area for hundreds of years. Their army had about 350,000 men. Roman soldiers were so good that no one beat them in battle for **500 years**. The Romans also ruled through fear and **intimidation**. In **73–71 B.C.**, an ex-gladiator named Spartacus led a slave revolt. The Romans captured the rebels and later executed them.

The End

Although historians say many factors led to Rome's demise, the beginning of the end was in **376–382 A.D.**, when the Romans fought a series of battles with the Goths, who invaded Rome from the north. By **476 A.D.**, the once-mighty empire was crushed.

The Roman Colosseum today

43 A.D.
Rome begins its conquest of Britain, and 80 years later, a wall was built separating the northern and southern parts of the country.

70–80 A.D.
The Romans build the Colosseum, one of the greatest stadiums in the ancient world.

285 A.D.
The Roman Empire splits into western and eastern regions.

WHEN Was the Great Wall of China Built?

The Great Wall of China was built about **2,500 years ago**. It is actually a series of walls that stretch for about 5,000 miles (8,047 km). China's first emperor connected several walls in the northern part of the country to defend against outside attacks. The Great Wall of China has been called the "longest cemetery on Earth" due to the number of people who died during its construction— possibly over 1 million. To save funeral and burial expenses, the bodies were buried in the wall.

Pounding Dirt

The Chinese built much of the wall by pounding dirt between board frames. Experts estimate that workers used roughly 393 million cubic yards of dirt during construction. They also built parts of the wall from brick and stone.

Who Were the Terracotta Warriors?

The **terracotta** warriors of China are life-sized clay soldiers. The 8,000 infantrymen, archers, generals, and cavalry were discovered in **1974** when farmers were digging a well near the city of Xian. The soldiers and their horses were found near the unexcavated tomb of Qin Shi Huangdi, who proclaimed himself the first emperor of China in **221 B.C.**

China's terracotta warriors

FUN FACTS

- More than **2,000 years ago**, a farmer in China tied a string to his hat to prevent it from blowing away, inventing the first kite.

- The Chinese believed that if they flew kites on the ninth day of the ninth month, they would ward off evil.

- In the Han Dynasty, General Huen Tsang used a kite designed like a pig to measure the distance from his army's position to his enemy's army. He wanted his troops to dig a tunnel, enter a palace, and end the siege. The enemy was so astounded to see a flying pig that they did not try to shoot the kite down with their flaming arrows.

Chinese fighting kite

WHEN Did It Happen in Beijing?

Beijing is both an ancient and a modern city, established more than **3,000 years ago**. The city became the capital of a united China in **1272**, during the Yuan Dynasty.

Forbidden Palace, Beijing

When Was the Forbidden City Built?

The Forbidden City in Beijing was built 600 years ago. It was once the imperial palace of Ming Dynasty rulers. Its now houses a museum.

The Boxer Rebellion

When Did the Boxer Rebellion Occur?

In 1900, the armies of several nations occupied Beijing during the Boxer Rebellion, when a group of Chinese Boxer fighters tried to force foreigners to leave the country.

When Did Communists Take Over China?

When Communists took over China from the nationalist government in 1949, they made Beijing the capital of the newly formed People's Republic of China. Communism is a form of government where a country's resources are shared and the government controls all of the property.

Mao Zedong, Chairman of the Chinese Communist Party

Mao Zedong meets with U.S. President Richard Nixon.

When Did Nixon Travel to China?

When Richard Nixon met with China's leader in Beijing in 1972, it was the first time a U.S. president had ever traveled to China.

When Did the Olympics Come to Beijing?

In 2008, Beijing hosted the Summer Olympic Games. The entire world watched as U.S. swimmer Michael Phelps won a record eight gold medals.

The Bird's Nest Olympic Stadium, the site of the opening ceremonies and track and field events

WHEN and Where Did the Earliest Civilizations in India Emerge?

India and its South Asian neighbors were home to some of the world's earliest civilizations, including the Indus, who thrived about 4,500 years ago along the Indus River in what is today Pakistan.

In the fertile Indus River Valley, small settlements developed into major cities. The Indus people traded pots and clothes made from cotton. The Indus Valley civilization stretched across a vast region including what is today Afghanistan, Pakistan, and northwestern India.

Irrigation Nation

Most members of the Indus Valley civilization were farmers who built elaborate irrigation systems to water their crops. They grew wheat, barley, peas, cotton, and rye. They traded these crops across Mesopotamia, located in modern-day Iraq.

Excavations at Mohenjo-Daro in current-day Pakistan reveal warehouses for storing grains and irrigation systems for watering fields.

The Mighty Guptas

The Guptas ruled northern and central India from 320 A.D. to 540 A.D. They were remarkable writers, artists, artisans, and musicians. One king, Samudra Gupta, was known for playing the harp and writing poetry. In 455, however, Huns from the north moved in and eventually destroyed the empire.

Nomads on the Go

Between 2000 and 1500 B.C., a group of nomads migrated from Europe and Asia into northwest India. Once they settled in India, these travelers began calling themselves Aryans.

The earliest Aryans were warriors who fought with bows and arrows and rode in chariots. The Aryans gradually settled down and built farming villages.

Statue of the Gupta god *Avalokiteshvara*, which means "the lord who looks upon the world with compassion"

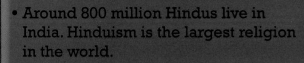

- Around 800 million Hindus live in India. Hinduism is the largest religion in the world.

- With 1.2 billion people, India has the second-largest population in the world. China holds the top spot.

- It took 20,000 workers 22 years to build the Taj Mahal, which Emperor Shah Jahan built in memory of his beloved wife, Mumtãz Mahal.

The Taj Mahal

WHEN Did the Maya Vanish?

More than **1,000 years ago**, the Maya created a great civilization in the jungles of Central America and southern Mexico. Their civilization flourished from about **250 A.D.** to **900 A.D.**, when they started leaving their cities and moving to small farming villages. Over time, their civilization vanished. Just why and how remains a mystery.

When Did the Maya First Appear?

The Maya first appeared on Mexico's Yucatan Peninsula nearly **6,000 years ago**, although no one seems to know where they came from. They built pyramids, studied **astronomy**, and had their own calendar. The Maya invented a form of writing comprised of **inscriptions** and pictures on wood and stone. They carved sculptures out of stone and clay. Mayan kings built great cities, including Tikal in Guatemala.

Mayan mask

Play Ball!

The Maya loved sports, particularly a game called the "ball game," which was played on a rectangular court bordered by two parallel walls built at an angle. Players had to pass a rubber ball through a circle located near the top of the wall using their hips, legs, feet, and arms—but not their hands. There is some evidence that those who lost the game were put to death.

Mayan ball court

Where Did They Go?

Scientists have various **theories** about the demise of Mayan culture. Some say a devastating **drought** doomed their civilization. Others say disease devastated their population. Some archaeologists speculate that a massive power struggle between rival cities engulfed the entire Mayan world, which resulted in the society's destruction. Today, descendants of the Maya cluster in Mexico, Belize, Guatemala, and Honduras.

Pyramid at Tikal, Guatemala

WHEN Did Humans Migrate from Africa?

The first modern humans came from Africa. Scientists believe our ancestors began migrating out of Africa 60,000 to 70,000 years ago. It is likely that Earth was cooling at that time, prompting people to move to warmer regions.

Where Did Everyone Go?

Some traveled north to Europe, while others ended up in Asia or Australia. Some crossed a land bridge between Asia and North America. From there, people migrated south to Central and South America. All these trips took time. It took at least a thousand years for people to migrate and settle in South America.

The Human Journey: Migration Routes

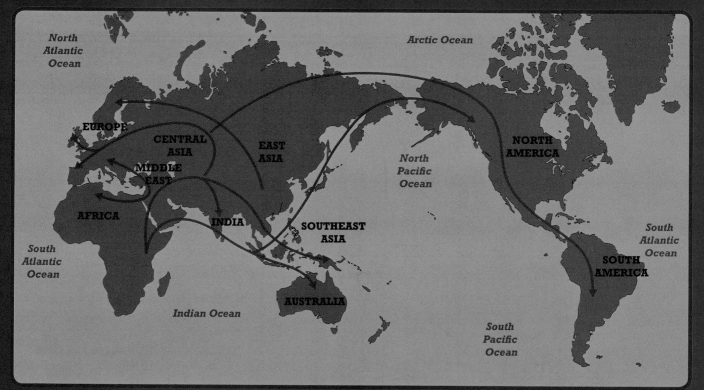

Sun temple of Ramses II in Nubia

Great Zimbabwe

Great Zimbabwe dominated life in East Africa in the 1300s. The word *zimbabwe* means "stone houses," which are a hallmark of the country. They were built to display the power of the king.

Africa's Early Civilizations

Nubia: Nubia, located in present-day Sudan, was also known as Kush. It was one of the great kingdoms of ancient Africa during the 7th and 8th centuries B.C. Its culture and religion were heavily influenced by Egypt.

Axum: Located on the coast of the Red Sea, Axum was a huge trading society. By 400 A.D., this kingdom had a network that connected Africa, India, and the Mediterranean world. Traders coming from the interior of the African continent brought ivory, animal hides, and gold to Axum. Those living along the coast brought iron, spices, and cotton cloth from India and beyond.

Obelisk erected in the 4th century, **Axum**

WHEN Were the First Olympics Held?

The Olympic Games took place in Greece in **776 B.C.** The Games were held as a festival to honor Zeus, the most powerful of the Greek gods. Unlike today's multi-sport Games, the first Olympics had only one event, a 210-yard (192 meter) foot race called the *stadion*. The winner of that first race was a cook named Koroibos.

Opening Ceremonies at the Olympic Winter Games, Sochi, Russia, 2014

No Women Allowed!

The ancient Olympic Games were held in Olympia, Greece. Packed with grand buildings and elaborate shrines, the temple of Zeus dominated the site. Only **Greek** males could participate in the ancient Games. While unmarried women were welcomed as spectators, married women were not allowed to play or watch. Today, women make up just under 50% of all Olympians.

Modern-Day Olympics

Today, there is great competition for the honor of hosting the Olympics. Recent host cities for the Winter Olympics include Sochi, Russia; Vancouver, Canada; and Turin, Italy. Summer Olympics have recently been held in London, England; Beijing, China; and Athens, Greece.

Tower Bridge during the 2012 **Olympics in London, England**

FU FACTS

At the 2012 Olympics, U.S. women won a total of 29 gold medals. If the U.S. women were their own country, they would have tied for third place with Great Britain for total gold medals.

Going for the Olive Wreath

Winners at the ancient Olympic Games received a crown made from olive branches, not medals. The tradition of giving medals began in 1896 and continues today. Originally, the top prize was a silver medal.

WHEN Was the First Baseball Game Played?

Abner Doubleday is credited with inventing the game in Cooperstown, New York, in 1839. But Americans may have been playing baseball long before that time.

Abner Doubleday

Who Won the First World Series?

The first World Series was played in 1903, when the Boston Americans—now known as the Boston Red Sox—beat the Pittsburgh Pirates. Before then, Major League Baseball had several championship games. One three-game series held in 1884 was called "The Championship of the United States." Newspapers named the winning team "World Champions," and the title stuck.

Fenway Park in Boston, Massachusetts

When Was Major League Baseball Established?

The first professional baseball team formed in 1869 in Cincinnati, Ohio. In 1876, the first major league, the National League, was formed, and the Western League followed in 1893. The American League, which grew out of the Western League, was not formed until 1901.

When Was the First Little League Game Played?

The very first Little League game was played on June 6, 1939, in Williamsport, Pennsylvania. Though Lundy Lumber hammered Lycoming Dairy, 23–8, Lycoming Dairy did not get discouraged. They came back from that lopsided loss and, at the end of the season, won in the best-of-three championship series.

More than 3 million kids play Little League.

A League of Their Own

In 1942, World War II (1939–1945) was in full swing. Many of Major League Baseball's greatest players went off to war. Fearing that baseball would collapse as a business, Phillip K. Wrigley, owner of the Chicago Cubs, helped create the All-American Girls Professional Baseball League. Women from across the United States got their chance to play professional ball. Many cities soon had teams of their own, including the Fort Wayne Daisies, the Racine Belles, and the Rockford Peaches.

Does a Curveball Curve?

Trying to hit a curveball, one of the most devastating pitches in baseball, is so difficult that it can make powerful Major League batters look like Little Leaguers. To understand this complicated pitch, you need to understand the **physics** of it.

In 2010 Aroldis Chapman, a Cincinnati Reds left-hander, made history by throwing the fastest pitch ever recorded in a Major League game, a 105-mph fastball.

Optical Illusion

Unlike a fastball, a curveball does not travel in a straight line. Instead, a curveball bends right or left as the ball moves up or down. At one time, most people thought it was nothing more than an optical illusion, but the naysayers were wrong.

Aroldis Chapman

Why Does It Curve?

At the heart of all curveballs is something called the Magnus effect, which has to do with air pressure rushing past the ball. Before a pitcher throws a curveball, he grips the ball with his middle and index fingers on or near the ball's stitching. He then places his thumb underneath the ball.

When the pitcher throws the ball, he twists his wrist as if he's turning a doorknob. As the ball spins and flies through the air, air pressure builds up on the stitches. That creates high air pressure on top of the ball and low air pressure underneath it. The higher air pressure pushes the ball toward where the air pressure is the lowest. This imbalance—the Magnus effect— causes the ball to curve toward one side.

FU FACTS

A good curveball can break, or appear to change direction, just 19 inches before it reaches the batter.

Higher air pressure

Flight path

Ball rotation

Lower air pressure

DID YOU KNOW?

Many people credit Fred Goldsmith with throwing the first curveball in the 1870s. Others say it was Candy Cummings in 1867. No matter who threw it first, the curveball changed the history of the game.

During his 21-year baseball career (1890–1911), Cy Young won more games than any other pitcher.

WHEN Did Racial Barriers Come Down in Professional Baseball?

For many years, because baseball was segregated, African Americans had their own leagues called the Negro Leagues. That changed in 1947, when Jackie Robinson, one of the "People Who Rocked the World" joined the Brooklyn Dodgers.

April 15, 1947, (from left to right), Brooklyn Dodgers baseball players John Jorgensen, Pee Wee Reese, Ed Stanky, and Jackie Robinson at Ebbets Field in New York

When African Americans began to play in the Major Leagues, fewer fans came to watch the Negro Leagues, which began to lose money. In response, women were hired to play in the Negro Leagues, and Toni Stone was the first ever signed by a professional men's team.

Oh, Henry!

Hank Aaron was one of the baseball players who left the Negro Leagues to play in the Major Leagues. In 1954, Aaron made his Major League debut with the Milwaukee Braves. In 1974, he surpassed Babe Ruth's home-run record and is ranked as one of baseball's Top 5 players for hits and runs.

Toni Stone, the first woman to play professional baseball, shakes hands with Joe Louis, heavyweight boxing champion of the world, in 1949.

People Who Rocked the World

Jackie Robinson

Jackie Robinson was the first black player in the modern Major Leagues. Brooklyn Dodgers' owner Branch Rickey asked Robinson to play for the team. He had the skills, and Rickey believed Robinson had the character to handle the pressure and scrutiny he would face.

Robinson played his first game in 1947 and won the National League Rookie of the Year Award that year. Despite suffering insults and racial taunts from both fans and players, Robinson became one of the best players of his era and paved the way for other African Americans to play in the Major Leagues.

WHEN Was the First Basketball Game Played?

On December 21, 1891, the first basketball game was played in Springfield, Massachusetts, at what is today Springfield College.

James Naismith was trying to keep male students at the Springfield YMCA Training School occupied during the cold winter months. Naismith attached half-bushel peach baskets to two poles in the Y's gymnasium. Each basket was 10 feet (3.05 meters) off the ground. Players tried to put a ball through the "hoops." The sport caught on quickly: it was introduced in France in 1893, in England in 1894, and in Japan in 1900.

When Was the First NBA Game Played?

On November 1, 1946, the New York Knickerbockers played the Toronto Huskies at Maple Leaf Gardens in Toronto. Fans taller than the tallest Husky, who stood 6 feet 8 inches, were admitted for free. According to reports, the crowd at the game numbered 7,090. Though free tickets were given out, no one in attendance was actually taller than 6 feet 8 inches.

Two weeks after the first NBA game in 1946, the New York Knicks squared off against the Detroit Falcons.

James Naismith invented basketball using peach baskets.

When Did Women Start Playing Professional Basketball?

In 1986, Nancy Lieberman joined the U.S. Basketball League team called the Springfield Fame, becoming the first woman to play professionally with men. Lieberman later joined the Long Island Knights and the Washington Generals.

The Women's Professional Basketball League was formed in 1978 and lasted three years. Its successor, the Women's Basketball Association, was founded in April 1996. The league's first games were played the following year. Since then, the league has grown from eight to 12 teams and has millions of fans.

Nancy Lieberman

YOU DON'T SAY!

Long before dunking became big, players shot the ball by planting their feet on the court and throwing it toward the basket with one or both hands. This was called a set shot. Today, players mostly shoot jump shots.

WHEN Was the First Super Bowl?

On **January 15, 1967,** the champions of the National Football League and the American Football League came together to play the NFL's first championship game. The game, which was played in Los Angeles, California, was called the AFL–NFL World Championship Game. The Green Bay Packers beat the Kansas City Chiefs 35–10.

Bart Starr of the Green Bay Packers leads his team to the first Super Bowl win.

What's in a Name?

Where did the Super Bowl get its name? When Lamar Hunt, then the owner of the Kansas City Chiefs, spied his daughter playing with a Super Ball, it inspired him to call the AFL–NFL World Championship Game the "Super Bowl."

Lamar Hunt

When Was One of the Most Famous Super Bowl Games Played?

For many fans, Super Bowl XXIII was the greatest Super Bowl ever. On **January 22, 1989**, in Miami, Florida, San Francisco 49ers' quarterback Joe Montana was cemented as one of the best quarterbacks of all time. The game began slowly, with the 49ers and the Cincinnati Bengals trading field goals. Late in the fourth quarter, the 49ers found themselves trailing the Bengals 16–13.

Joe Cool

With just three minutes left in the game, the 49ers got the ball on their own 8-yard line. They had to march 92 yards downfield to score a touchdown. Joe Montana **orchestrated** an 11-play drive that drove fans wild. With only 39 seconds left in the game, he threw a touchdown pass to John Taylor, who had already made it to the end zone. The touchdown gave San Francisco the lead for good. Later, 49ers' coach Bill Walsh commented that it was Joe Montana at his best. Once again, he had lived up to his nickname, "Joe Cool."

Joe Montana led the San Francisco 49ers to a thrilling win in Super Bowl XXIII.

TRY IT!

Below are Joe Montana's statistics for Super Bowl XXIII. He completed 23 passes (CP) in 36 attempts (AT) for a total of 357 yards (YRDS). He threw two touchdowns (TD) and no interceptions (INT). How many yards did Montana average per pass? Hint: Divide the number of pass attempts into the number of yards. What was Montana's completion rate? Hint: Divide the number of completions into the number of passing attempts.

Passing	CP/AT	YRDS	TD	INT
Joe Montana	23/36	357	2	0

WHEN Were Other Historic Sports Moments?

The world of sports never stands still. Old records are broken, new records are created, and athletes set milestones every season. Here are a few more amazing moments worth cheering for.

U.S. athlete Maxwell Long won the gold medal in the men's 400 meter race at the 1900 Summer Olympics.

Major Moments in Sports

1900	1973	1977	1980
Summer Olympic Games, Paris, France	Kentucky Derby, Louisville, Kentucky	Indianapolis 500, Indiana	Winter Olympic Games, Lake Placid, New York

"He couldn't have moved faster if he had fallen off the grandstand roof," was one reaction when Secretariat captured the Triple Crown of horse racing by winning the Belmont Stakes. After wins at the Kentucky Derby and Preakness, Secretariat ran the Belmont's 1½-mile course in 2 minutes and 24 seconds.

Lightning Speed

You Go Girl!

Janet Guthrie became the first woman to race in the Indianapolis 500. The next year, she finished in ninth place.

U.S. Hockey Gold

During the 1980 Winter Olympics in Lake Placid, New York, the underdog U.S. hockey team faced the best hockey team in the world, the Soviet Union. The Soviets had won the Olympic gold medal in hockey four times in a row and outscored their opponents 175–44. On February 22, 1980, the U.S. team beat the Soviets 4–3, then went on to defeat Finland to win the gold medal.

Soccer Victory

In what some consider the greatest moment in U.S. soccer history, American Abby Wambach scored a dramatic goal against Brazil in the   Women's World Cup quarterfinal to tie Brazil 2–2 at the end of overtime. The U.S. won the match on penalty kicks.

1988
Summer Olympic Games, Seoul, South Korea

2011
FIFA Women's Soccer World Cup, Germany

2014
Winter Olympic Games, Sochi, Russia

Good as Gold
Mikaela Shiffrin won gold for the U.S. in Women's Slalom.

Gold medal winner Florence Griffith Joyner, also known as Flo-Jo, was an American track and field athlete. She is considered the fastest woman of all time.

Glossary

accuracy the quality or degree of correctness

acidic forming or containing a liquid that breaks down matter faster than water

aeronautics the science of flight

amphibious designed for use on both land and water

amphitheaters buildings with seats rising in curved rows around an open space on which games and plays take place

antenna a metal device used to send or receive signals such as radio waves

anthropology the study of human behavior, beliefs, and society

antiquity ancient times, especially the time period before the Middle Ages

architecture the art or science of designing and constructing structures such as homes and public buildings

artisans craftsmen; people who work with their hands in the production or repair of material items

assembly line an arrangement of machines, equipment, and workers in which work passes from operation to operation in a direct line until the product is assembled

astronomy field of science that studies the sun, planets, moons, and stars

authorize give permission, make legal

axis a line upon which an object turns or seems to turn

balance a condition in which opposing forces are equal to each other

barbarians uncivilized people

brainchild an idea, plan, or creation of one person

bubonic plague a serious illness that is usually spread by fleas and that often leads to death

bushel a unit of measurement of dry goods; a large amount

calculations the act of solving or the results of a mathematical problem

cargo the load of goods carried by an airplane, ship, or automobile

cartridges cases for holding things that are awkward to handle, such as integrated circuits containing computer programs

civilizations highly developed cultures

colonize to settle in a new land and claim it for the government of another country

combustion an act or instance of burning

comet heavenly body made of ice and dust, which has a tail and an unusual path around the sun

constellation a group of stars

control to direct the action of

crude existing in a natural state and unaltered by cooking or processing

Crusades wars begun by European Christians who tried to take back the Holy Land from the Muslims in the 11th–13th centuries

debuted made a first public appearance

deciphered interpreted the meaning of

dimension the length, width, or height of an object

domesticated raised to live with people

drought a long period of dry weather

electromagnet a magnet made by electricity

engineer a person whose job is to plan and build engines, machines, roads, or bridges

enticing attracting by arousing hope or desire

escapement the part of a clock that keeps it ticking in an even rhythm

evolved changed over many years

experimental relating to a scientific testing

extinct no longer existing

extraterrestrial coming from or existing outside the Earth or its atmosphere

filaments single threads or thin, flexible, threadlike parts

fossils traces, prints, or hardened remains of plants or animals

friction the act of rubbing one thing against another

gargantuan very large in size or amount

generator a machine that makes electrical energy

geyser an explosion of liquid and steam from a crack in Earth's surface

gliders aircraft that fly on air currents and have no motor

gravity the natural force that causes objects to move toward the center of Earth

grindstone a stone disk that turns on an axle and is used for grinding or sharpening

habitable suitable or fit to live in

hibernate to spend the winter in a sleeping or resting state

hydrogen a colorless gas that burns easily and weighs less than any other known matter

hypertext transfer protocol (http) a method of controlling the exchange of computer data, especially on the World Wide Web

iceberg a very large piece of ice that has detached from a glacier and is floating in the water

illuminated brightened with light

illusion a misleading image presented to the eye

immigrants people who have moved to a new country

inception an important point in progress or development; the beginning

Industrial Revolution a time in history beginning in the mid-1700s, when power-driven machines were first used to produce goods in large quantities, changing the way people lived and worked

inscriptions words that are written or cut into something

intentional done on purpose; not accidental

interstellar located among the stars

intimidation using threats to scare someone into doing what you want

jargon the special language of a particular activity or group

leap day the extra day in a leap year, February 29, occurring every four years

legend a story passed down through the years that cannot be proven

lenses clear, curved pieces of material such as glass used to bend rays of light to form images, especially to correct vision or magnify an object

lift an upward force (as on an airplane wing) that opposes the pull of gravity

magnetism the force that pulls certain objects toward a magnet

mass production the method of making things in large quantities

meteoroid a chunk of rock or ice that revolves around the sun

Middle Ages the period of European history from about 500 A.D. to about 1500

migrate to move from one country or place to another

milestones important points in progress or development

molecules the smallest bits of matter possible before they can be broken down into their basic parts

moorings places or objects to which a boat or aircraft can be fastened

mythology a collection of stories dealing with the gods and heroes of a particular people

networks systems of computers connected by communication lines

neutron a particle with a neutral electric charge found in the nucleus of an atom

nuclear reactor machine in which nuclear power is safely created

nuclei the central parts of atoms that include nearly all of their atomic mass and consist of protons and (usually) neutrons

nutrient food that a living thing needs to live and grow

operator a person who performs a particular task

orchestrated arranged, set up

parchment the hide of an animal that was prepared to be used as paper

patent a document that stops people from copying an invention and gives the inventor the legal right to prevent others from making, using, or selling that invention

pendulum part of a clock hung from a fixed point that swings freely back and forth under the action of gravity

pharaohs ancient Egyptian rulers

pistons sliding pieces in engines that move up and down inside cylinders as they make power

portable easy to carry or move around

predator an animal that kills other animals for food

prey an animal hunted or killed by another animal for food

primitive something that is in an early stage of growth; something from the ancient past

probe a vessel that is sent to do advanced studies in an environment before people are sent in

prototypes the first models on which later models are developed or based

quill a pen made from a feather

radiation a dangerous, powerful energy that is produced by radioactive substances and nuclear reactions; rays of light, heat, or energy that spread outward

radio waves waves that are carried by changes in both electric and magnetic fields that include those waves used to carry radio and television signals

resin a sticky liquid from the gum or sap of some trees

rotation one complete turn

scribes people who copied books by hand

solo something that is done alone

species a single kind of living thing (all people are one species)

speculation thoughts or guesses about something

staple an important and basic food item; something that is in constant demand

synchronize to make things happen at the same time

taunts sarcastic comments, insults

terracotta a type of brownish orange clay often used to make statues and vases

theories ideas that try to explain something

time zones geographic regions within which the same standard time is used

tolling ringing of a bell

tombs buildings or chambers above or below the ground in which dead bodies are kept

transportable something that can be carried from one place to another

understatement presenting something as being less important than it is

vacuum tubes electron tubes from which most of the air has been removed

vendors people or stores that sell goods

warships military ships that are armed for combat

Index

Credits

Front cover: Bad Man Production/ Shutterstock.com
Back cover: Umberto Shtanzman/ Shutterstock.com (smartphones); M. Unal Ozmen/Shutterstock.com (ice cream); Arcaid/UIG/Getty Images (clock tower)
P 5: © DIZ Muenchen GmbH, Sueddeutsche Zeitung Photo/Alamy (watching TV); dtopal/Shutterstock. com (look back); haveseen/ Shutterstock.com (look forward); Donna Ward/Getty Images (Jimmy Fallon); © Bettmann/CORBIS (1940); gallofoto/Shutterstock.com (1950); NotarYES/Shutterstock.com (1960); Rockworth/Shutterstock.com (1970); trekandshoot/Shutterstock. com (1980); Dmitry Naumov/ Shutterstock.com (1990); maggee/ Shutterstock.com (2000); Tungphoto/ Shutterstock.com (2010)
pp 6–7: Matt Cardy/Getty Images (clock); Alex Hubenov/Shutterstock. com (sun clock dial); f9photos/ Shutterstock.com (hourglass)
pp 8–9: Jose Ignacio Soto/Shutterstock. com (Egyptian calendar); Kudinovart/ Dreamstime (Mayan calendar); Prisma/ UIG/Getty Images (Gregory XII)
pp 10–11: Neil Wigmore/Shutterstock. com (sundial); David Carillet/ Shutterstock.com (moon phases); fotosutra.com/Shutterstock.com (Milky Way)
pp 12–13: SSPL/Getty Images (water-balance escapement); Andrey Burmakin/Shutterstock.com (hourglass); OZaiachin/Shutterstock. com (candle)
pp 14–15: Christoph Schissler/Walters Art Museum (Portable Drum Watch); Galushko Sergey/Shutterstock.com (device); Arcaid/UIG/Getty Images (clock tower)
pp 16–17: Sashkin/Shutterstock.com (world stopwatch); Faded Beauty/ Shutterstock.com (locomotive); © CORBIS (poster)
pp 18–19: © Roger Bamber/Alamy (International Meridian monument); Andrea Izzotti/Shutterstock.com (tonga); De Agostini Picture Library/ IndiaPicture (Ferdinand Magellan Sabrosa)
pp 20–21: Antonio M. Rosario/Getty Images (Pluto); JPL/NASA (Neptune); Science Photo Library—ANDRZEJ WOJCICKI/Brand X Pictures/ Getty Images (Mars); Denis Tabler/ Shutterstock.com (Earth); parameter/ Getty Images (Mercury); NASA/JPL (Venus); NASA/JPL/University of Arizona (Jupiter); NASA/JPL/Space Science Institute (Saturn); SSPL/Getty Images (Uranus); CLAUS LUNAU/

Science Photo Library/Getty Images (solar system)
pp 22–23: Csu Archives/Everett Collection/IndiaPicture (time capsule); jeff gynane/Shutterstock.com (sign); ALFREDO ESTRELLA/AFP/Getty Images (Yahoo)
pp 24–25: Karen Doody/Stocktrek Images/Getty Images
pp 26–27: © Jonathan Blair/Corbis (fossil); Danita Delimont/Gallo Images/Getty Images (alligator); Mathee Suwannarak/Shutterstock. com (crocodile); Eric Isselee/ Shutterstock.com (American alligator)
pp 28–29: Dariush M/Shutterstock. com (dinosaur doomsday); Michael Rosskothen/Shutterstock.com (Triassic); Encyclopedia Britannica/ UIG/Getty Images (Jurassic); DM7/ Shutterstock.com (Cretaceous)
pp 30–31: O. Louis Mazzatenta/ National Geographic/Getty Images (fossil); Glenn Bartley/Getty Images (hummingbird); Targn Pleiades/ Shutterstock.com (bird); KellyNelson/ Shutterstock.com (flowers); Michael Rosskothen/Shutterstock.com (*caudipteryx*)
pp 32–33: Delmas Lehman/ Shutterstock.com (geese); Sally Wallis/ Shutterstock.com (blue bird); Cico/ Shutterstock.com (screw)
pp 34–35: DarZel/Shutterstock. com (wolf); Capture Light/ Shutterstock.com (Labrador retriever); Nataliya_Ostapenko/Shutterstock. com (German shepherd); Jan S/ Shutterstock.com (golden retriever); siloto/Shutterstock.com (beagle); RAYphotographer/Shutterstock.com (bulldog); Image Broker/IndiaPicture (Great Dane)
pp 36–37: Africa Studio/Shutterstock. com (kitten); FloraStyles/Shutterstock. com (cat); © Steve Vidler/Alamy/ IndiaPicture (Egyptian mummified cat)
pp 38–39: Manoj Shah/The Image Bank/Getty Images (baboon); JOSEPH NETTIS/Getty Images (rhinoceros); Library of Congress (Theodore Roosevelt)
pp 40–41: © moodboard/Corbis (crowd); Elena Larina/Shutterstock. com (dolphins); Robert Harding/ IndiaPicture (cave painting); Lonely Planet/Getty Images (newspapers)
pp 42–43: DEA/G. DAGLI ORTI/De Agostini/Getty Images (clay tablet); Buena Vista Images/Photodisc/ Getty Images (stop signal); cobalt88/ Shutterstock.com (Egyptian papyrus); Fotosearch/Getty Images (Rosetta stone); Leemage/UIG/Getty Images (Jean-Francois Champollion)
p 44: SSPL/Getty Images (Gutenberg

press); © Peter Horree/Alamy/ IndiaPicture (Gutenberg Bible)
pp 46–47: Ensuper/Shutterstock. com (Morse key); Hulton Archive/ Getty Images (Samuel Morse); © Ilene MacDonald/Alamy/IndiaPicture (Morse code)
pp 48–49: Fox Photos/Getty Images (Alexander Bell); Nagel Photography/ Shutterstock.com (1907); Mike Flippo/ Shutterstock.com (1919); stockphoto-graf/Shutterstock.com (1934); ARENA Creative/Shutterstock.com (1954); Giulio_Fornasar/Shutterstock.com (1982); Galushko Sergey/Shutterstock. com (2014); Alexander Graham Bell/ The Bridgeman Art Library/Getty Images (look back); Albert Llop/ Anadolu Agency/Getty Images (look forward)
pp 50–51: Mary/IndiaPicture (Guglielmo Marconi); © Hulton-Deutsch Collection/CORBIS (Radio Aerial); William James Warren/Science Faction/Getty Images (antenna); R. Gino Santa Maria/Shutterstock.com (1930); stockphoto-graf/Shutterstock. com (1960); Avesun/Shutterstock.com (2000); You can more/Shutterstock. com (2014)
pp 52–53: © DIZ Muenchen GmbH, Sueddeutsche Zeitung Photo/Alamy (watching TV); dtopal/Shutterstock. com (look back); haveseen/ Shutterstock.com (look forward); Donna Ward/Getty Images (Jimmy Fallon); © Bettmann/CORBIS (1940); gallofoto/Shutterstock.com (1950); NotarYES/Shutterstock.com (1960); Rockworth/Shutterstock.com (1970); trekandshoot/Shutterstock.com (1980); Dmitry Naumov/Shutterstock.com (1990); maggee/Shutterstock.com (2000); Tungphoto/Shutterstock.com (2010)
pp 54–55: Blend Images – KidStock/ Brand X Pictures/Getty Images (family); Levranii/Shutterstock.com (child); SEBASTIAN DERUNGS/ AFP/Getty Images (Tim Berners-Lee); Joe McNally/Getty Images (Bill Gates)
pp 56–57: © Xu Yu/Xinhua Press/ Corbis (wooden movable types); Anton Balazh/Shutterstock.com (Earth); SSPL/Getty Images (Michael Faraday); SSPL/Getty Images (echo)
pp 58–59: SSPL/Getty Images (Montgolfier balloon); LittleStocker/ Shutterstock.com (hot air balloon); Universal History Archive/Getty Images (balloon flight); ASSOCIATED PRESS (lawnchair balloonist); John B. Carnett/Bonnier Corp./Getty Images (Steve Fosset)
pp 60–61: SSPL/Getty Images (Wilbur

and Orville Wright); Photononstop RM/IndiaPicture (sculpture); ASSOCIATED PRESS (Gustave Whitehead)
pp 62–63: MO_SES Premium/ Shutterstock.com (plane); ©Historic Florida/Alamy/IndiaPicture (benoist)
pp 64–65: New York Times Co./Getty Images (Lindbergh And Spirit); ASSOCIATED PRESS (Amelia Earhart)
pp 66–67: Popperfoto/Getty Images (*Hindenburg*); Dorling Kindersley/ Getty Images(Cut-away); NY Daily News Archive/Getty Images (*Hindenburg*)
pp 68–69: ASSOCIATED PRESS (Charles Yeager); Erik Simonsen/ Photographer's Choice/Getty Images (SR-71 Blackbird); Apic/Getty Images (look back)
pp 70–71: AFP/Getty Images (Yuri Gagarin); NASA (Alan Shepard); Everett/IndiaPicture (John Glenn); ASSOCIATED PRESS (Valentina Tereshkova); nienora/Shutterstock. com (night sky)
pp 72–73: NASA (Mars rover); NASA/ JPL-Caltech/Cornell/NMMNH (Mars); NASA/JPL-Caltech/University of Arizona (*Viking* lander); Paramount Pictures/Getty Images (movie poster)
pp 74–75: NASA/Newsmakers (Apollo 11); NASA (lunar module); Sovfoto/ UIG/Getty Images (look back); pockygallery/Shutterstock.com (look forward)
pp 76–77: altrendo images/Stockbyte/ Getty Images (family); Science Picture Co/Getty Images (*Homo erectus*); TOM MCHUGH/Photo Researchers/ Getty Images (*Neanderthal*); Barbara Strnadova/Photo Researchers/ Getty Images (nutcracker man); Science Picture Co/Getty Images (evolution)
pp 78–79: Pecold/Shutterstock.com (water mill); ChinaFotoPress/ ChinaFotoPress/Getty Images (Three Gorges Dam); © Eddie Gerald/Alamy/ IndiaPicture (model)
pp 80–81: Hulton Archive/Getty Images (Benjamin Franklin); © Roger Coulam/Alamy/IndiaPicture (lighting); Molodec/Shutterstock.com (electric flash)
pp 82–83: Freer/Shutterstock.com (candle); ©Ambient Images Inc./ Alamy/IndiaPicture (Gateway Arch Gaslamp)
pp 84–85: FPG/Getty Images (Colonel Drake); Boyer/Roger Viollet/ Getty Images (oil well); r.classen/ Shutterstock.com (gasoline); © CORBIS (oil Gushing)
pp 86–87: Johan Ramberg/Getty

Images (photons); fotohunter/ Shutterstock.com (solar panel); Universal History Archive/Getty Images (look back); Scott Barbour/ Getty Images (look forward); © Car Culture/Corbis (car)

pp 88–89: DIETER NAGL/AFP/Getty Images (reactor core); Martin Lisner/ Shutterstock.com (nuclear power plant); Sovfoto/UIG/Getty Images (Marie Curie)

pp 90–91: Radius Images/Getty Images (windmills); Jeffrey Liao/Shutterstock. com (Nile); moodboard/Brand X Pictures/Getty Images (windmills)

pp 92–93: Mopic/Shutterstock.com (earth); Mopic/Shutterstock.com (sun); Chad Baker/Stockbyte/Getty Images (sunspots)

pp 94–95: solarseven/Shutterstock. com (meteor); Vadim Sadovski/ Shutterstock.com (Earth); Knorre/ Shutterstock.com (bacteria); Dr. T.J. Beveridge/Visuals Unlimited/Getty Images (extremophiles); Kenneth Keifer/Shutterstock.com (organism)

pp 96–97: NASA/JPL-Caltech (orion); Image Work/amanaimagesRF/Getty Images (astrology sign); NASA/CXC/ STScI/JPL-Caltech/UIUC/Univ. of Minn (N49); Roth Sanford/Photo Researchers/Getty Images (Edwin Hubble)

pp 98–99: Science Photo Library— ANDRZEJ WOJCICKI/Brand X Pictures/Getty Images (asteroid); Paul Fleet/Shutterstock.com (comet); YURI KADOBNOV/AFP/Getty Images (meteor)

pp 100–101: NASA/JPL (*Voyager* spacecraft); NASA/JPL (voyager 2); NASA (Jupiter); NASA/JPL (Saturn); NASA/JPL (Neptune)

pp 102–103: Gianni Tortoli/Photo Researchers/Getty Images (Galileo Telescope); Universal/IndiaPicture (Galileo); Detlev van Ravensweaay/ Picture Press/Getty Images (Kepler telescope)

pp 104–105: ©INTERFOTO/Alamy/ IndiaPicture (Zuse); US Army/Photo Researchers/Getty Images (circuit boards); Timothy Hodgkinson/ Shutterstock.com (CPU); MixAll Studio/Blend Images/Getty Images (digital display)

pp 106–107: © Ed Quinn/Corbis (Ray Tomlinson); © Design Pics Inc./Alamy/ IndiaPicture (computer); vectorlib. com (server); Reto Stöckli, Nazmi El Saleous, and Marit Jentoft-Nilsen, NASA GSFC (Earth)

pp 108–109: Image Source/Getty Images (friends); Sauromatum Design/Shutterstock.com (messaging); Bilgin S. Sasmaz/Anadolu Agency/ Getty Images (Twitter); TRINACRIA PHOTO/Shutterstock.com (football)

pp 110–111: Bruce Rolff/Shutterstock. com (screens); © Frances Roberts/ Alamy/IndiaPicture (HDTV Studio);

adventtr/Vetta/Getty Images (3D movie)

pp 112–113: PHILIPPE HUGUEN/ AFP/Getty Images (smartphones); ©shinypix/Alamy/IndiaPicture (1991); ©Radharc Images/Alamy/IndiaPicture (1994); SSPL/Getty Images (2000); Ted Thai/Time Life Pictures/Getty Images (2002); ASSOCIATED PRESS (2004); ©Jacek Lasa/Alamy/IndiaPicture (2014); Justin Sullivan/Getty Images (Steve Jobs)

pp 114–115: Suzanne Kreiter/The Boston Globe/Getty Images (Ralph Baer); © INTERFOTO/Alamy/ IndiaPicture (Video Game); Image Source/Getty Images (teenage boys); © David L. Moore—Lifestyle/Alamy (Nintendo Wii)

pp 116–117: © Stephen Sweet/Alamy/ IndiaPicture (cutaway); © Dunca Daniel Mihai/Alamy/IndiaPicture (woman); © Bernhard Classen/Alamy/ IndiaPicture (pixels)

pp 118–119: The Asahi Shimbun/Getty Images (H-IIB); © Corbis (Kirobo); Ulrich Baumgarten/Getty Images (production); ©Mike Stone/Alamy/ IndiaPicture (robot)

pp 120–121: jose marques lopes/ Shutterstock.com (plantation); Foodio/ Shutterstock.com (popcorn); Library of Congress (Thanksgiving)

pp 122–123: © INTERFOTO/Alamy/ IndiaPicture (Alexander); M. Unal Ozmen/Shutterstock.com (ice-cream); Stock Montage/Getty Images (Dolley Madison); Stuart Dee/Photographer's Choice RF/Getty Images (flavors)

pp 124–125: effe45/Shutterstock.com (peanuts); Madlen/Shutterstock.com (peanut butter); © whiteboxmedia limited/Alamy/IndiaPicture (skippy); Stock Montage/Getty Images (G W Carver)

pp 126–127: Print Collector/Getty Images (Margherita of Savoy); vsl/ Shutterstock.com (pizza)

pp 128–129: Universal/IndiaPicture (John Montagu); Ann Ronan Pictures/Print Collector/Getty Images (spinning cotton); Nattika/ Shutterstock.com (hamburger); Lu Mikhaylova/Shutterstock.com (Sandwich)

pp 130–131: Madlen/Shutterstock. com (lollipop); © Ian Dagnall/Alamy (chocolate); © Michael Ventura/ Alamy/IndiaPicture (Hershey); Alamy/ IndiaPicture (M&M's)

pp 132–133: Photononstop RM/ IndiaPicture (restaurant); gresei/ Shutterstock.com (hamburger); ©B. Leighty/Photri Images/Alamy/ IndiaPicture (franchise); © Franck Fotos/Alamy/IndiaPicture (statue)

pp 134–135: © pf/Alamy/IndiaPicture (Hot Dog Stand); Alex459/Shutterstock. com (hot dog); Tim Boyle/Getty Images (Oscar Mayer Wieners)

pp 136–137: Stock Montage/Getty

Images (Robert Fulton); © North Wind Picture Archives/Alamy/IndiaPicture (Clermont); © Hemis/Alamy/ IndiaPicture (Natchez); Kenneth Vincent Summers/Shutterstock.com (USS *Nimitz*)

pp 138–139: © National Geographic Image Collection/Alamy/IndiaPicture (*Titanic*); © Niday Picture Library/ Alamy/IndiaPicture (*Lusitania*); Loomis Dean/Time Life Pictures/Getty Images (*Andrea Doria*)

pp 140–141: Mondadori Portfolio/Getty Images (Gottlieb Daimler); ©MARKA/ Alamy/IndiaPicture (Felix Millet Motorcycle); Blend RF/IndiaPicture (Dirt Bike); Margo Harrison/ Shutterstock.com (Motocross Bike)

pp 142–143: © Bettmann/CORBIS (race); anyaivanova/Shutterstock. com (look back); Oleksiy Mark/ Shutterstock.com (look forward); Ortodox/Shutterstock.com (train)

pp 144–145: Culture Club/Hulton Archive/Getty Images (automobile); ©Stan Rohrer/Alamy/IndiaPicture (Ford); Fotosearch/Getty Images (assembly line); Mondadori Portfolio/ Getty Images (Karl Benz)

pp 146–147: © Dennis Cox/Alamy/ IndiaPicture (Cathedral Of Junk); ©Andrew Shinn/Alamy/IndiaPicture (restaurant); Image Source/ IndiaPicture (drive-in)

pp 148–149: Age fotostock (pixtal)/ IndiaPicture (stamp); Photo Researchers/Getty Images (golden spike); Tim Roberts Photography/ Shutterstock.com (stack); © Bruno Morandi/Corbis (train)

pp 150–151: © ZUMA Press, Inc./ Alamy/IndiaPicture (skycar); ©Annette Price—H2O Photography/ Alamy/IndiaPicture (aquada); ©Iain Masterton/Alamy/IndiaPicture (car)

pp 152–153: Richard Nowitz/Getty Images (Tutankhamun); ©Gavin Hellier/Alamy/IndiaPicture (Egypt)

pp 154–155: © Peter Horree/ Alamy/IndiaPicture (Melpomene); Anastasios71/Shutterstock.com (Parthenon); Morphart Creation/ Shutterstock.com (Trojan horse); Ann Ronan Pictures/Print Collector/ Getty Images (Pandora); Encyclopedia Britannica/UIG/Getty Images (King Midas)

pp 156–157: © INTERFOTO/Alamy/ IndiaPicture (coin); Veronika Galkina/ Shutterstock.com (Colosseum); Algol/ Shutterstock.com (soldier)

pp 158–159: imageshunter/ Shutterstock.com (Great Wall); James Montgomery/Getty Images (terracotta warriors); davidelliottphotos/ Shutterstock.com (kite)

pp 160–161: Jixin YU/Shutterstock.com (taihe palace); Leemage/UIG/Getty Images (rebels); AFP/Getty Images (Mao Zedong); Sovfoto/UIG/Getty Images (Mao & Nixon); © Xiaoyang

Liu/Corbis (stadium)

pp 162–163: Ursula Gahwiler/ Robert Harding/Getty Images (Mohenjodaro); © Burstein Collection/ CORBIS (statue); Dmitry Strizhakov/ Shutterstock.com (Taj Mahal)

pp 164–165: © Alberto Masnovo/ Alamy/IndiaPicture (God mask); Mark Yarchoan/Shutterstock.com (Tikal); De Agostini Picture Library/IndiaPicture (Honduras)

pp 166–167: Stephen Studd/Getty Images (Sun temple); 2630ben/ Shutterstock.com (Great Zimbabwe); Martin Harvey/Photolibrary/Getty Images (stele)

pp 168–169: Robert Beck/Sports Illustrated/Getty Images (winter Olympics); 169: AWL RM/IndiaPicture (tower bridge)

pp 170–171: © ArtPix/Alamy/ IndiaPicture (Abner Doubleday); Mark Rucker/Transcendental Graphics/Getty Images (Boston Red Sox); ©LOOK Die Bildagentur der Fotografen GmbH/Alamy/ IndiaPicture (stadium); Christina Lease/Lonely Planet Images/Getty Images (baseball); © Bettmann/ CORBIS (baseball players)

pp 172–173: Chuck Solomon/Sports Illustrated/Getty Images (Aroldis Chapman); iymsts/Shutterstock.com (ball); © Bettmann/CORBIS (Cy Young)

pp 174–175: ASSOCIATED PRESS (Jackie Robinson Movie Baseball); © Bettmann/CORBIS (Hank Aaron); © Minnesota Historical Society/ CORBIS (Toni & Joe); MLB Photos/ Hulton Archive/ Getty Images(Jackie Robinson)

pp 176–177: © Bettmann/CORBIS (Dr. Naismith); © Bettmann/CORBIS (rebound ball); © George Tiedemann/ Corbis (Nancy Lieberman); ©McClatchy-Tribune Information Services/Alamy/IndiaPicture (Stephen Curry)

pp 178–179: Neil Leifer/Sports Illustrated/Getty Images (Super Bowl I); Joe Ledford/Kansas City Star/ MCT/Getty Images (Lamar Hunt); TRINACRIA PHOTO/Shutterstock. com (football); Mike Powell/Getty Images (Joe Montana)

pp 180–181: Popperfoto/Getty Images (Maxwell "Maxey"); Focus On Sport/ Getty Images (Belmont Stakes); ISC Archives/Getty Images (Janet Guthrie); Steve Powell/Getty Images (1980); NBC/Getty Images (Florence Griffith-Joyner); Martin Rose/Getty Images (Abby Wambach); Simon Bruty/Sports Illustrated/Getty Images (Mikaela Shiffrin)

Maps: Created by Contentra Technologies
Artwork: Created by Contentra Technologies